GREEN MY HOME!

D0870909

GREEN MY HOME!

10 Steps to Lowering Energy Costs and Reducing Your Carbon Footprint

By Dennis C. Brewer

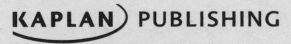

KAPLAN PUBLISHING

New York

This publication is designed to provide accurate and authoritative information in regard to the subject matter covered. It is sold with the understanding that the publisher is not engaged in rendering legal, accounting, or other professional service. If legal advice or other expert assistance is required, the services of a competent professional should be sought.

Published by Kaplan Publishing, a division of Kaplan, Inc.
1 Liberty Plaza, 24th Floor
New York, NY 10006

Printed in the United States of America

Library of Congress Cataloging-in-Publication Data

Brewer, Dennis C., 1949-
  Green my home! : 10 steps to lowering energy costs and reducing
  your carbon footprint / Dennis C. Brewer.
    p. cm.
  ISBN 978-1-4277-9841-1 (pbk.)
  1. Dwellings—Energy conservation. 2. Ecological houses.
3. Environmental protection—Citizen participation. 4. Sustainable
living. I. Title.
  TJ163.5.D86B74 2008
  644—dc22   2008025256

10 9 8 7 6 5 4 3 2 1

ISBN-13: 978-1-4277-9841-1

Kaplan Publishing books are available at special quantity discounts to use for sales promotions, employee premiums, or educational purposes. Please email our Special Sales Department to order or for more information at kaplanpublishing@kaplan.com, or write to Kaplan Publishing, 1 Liberty Plaza, 24th Floor, New York, NY 10006.

Contents

Contents

Contents

Contents

Introduction:
What Does It Really Mean
to Be Living Green in the
New Millennium?

Our definition of what "getting green" or "going green" really means needs to reach a common understanding. It is not all green apples; there are some hot peppers to consider in the mix. Over the next few paragraphs, a distinction is made to clarify the important differences between the two categories of environmental actions and activism that are often presented under the same banner of "being green."

Pervasive and Surprising Sources of Air Pollution

Who would have ever guessed that eating cheeseburgers could be polluting more in the form of greenhouse gases than driving your SUV? In America our collective appetite for hamburgers may very well contribute as much as 200 million metric tons of carbon (CO_2 equivalent) into the atmosphere. In the same way we infrequently think about the pollution contribution from what we eat for lunch, we don't often think about how much carbon pollution we contribute to the atmosphere simply from our living arrangements: our homes or apartments. Not only do these things add to the difficult-to-solve problems in our environment, every pound of *unnecessary* carbon dioxide pollution also wastes money while providing *no useful benefit*. Every time you use energy or cause energy to be used on your behalf, you are adding carbon to the atmosphere.

Current Rates of Carbon-Based Household Energy Consumption Are Too High

Much of the discussion and media attention over the last decade has been about saving the environment by reducing the negative environmental impact of our personal transportation preferences. There is little doubt that our transportation choices can make a substantial difference in the amount of pollution we generate by our daily living activities. We buy cars and we personally live with that choice, typically for as long as three to five years. Whether we choose a gas guzzler or gas miser, the time period it impacts our pocketbooks is very short compared to our choices for living arrangements. Many people live in their homes for 30 years or a whole lifetime. How we choose to consume energy at home every day adds up steadily to surprising levels of greenhouse gas emissions. If one examines the environmental impact of our collective choices in the residential sector for energy consumption here in the United States, the numbers for greenhouse gas emissions are alarming. What we see is the energy bill in dollars and cents, typically $200 to $400 a month per household for electricity and heating fuel combined. This shifts our focus away from the real problem: excess carbon dioxide and other greenhouse gases being released into the atmosphere directly from our homes or on our behalf at fossil fuel powered electric generation plants. To put this in perspective, I looked to U.S. Department of Energy publications, as their ability to collect statistics is often impressive. What I found was alarming beyond expectations. According to a U.S. Department of Energy's Energy Information Administration report covering the year 2006, the United States is considered to be contributing 22 percent of the total greenhouse gases worldwide. We are said to be responsible for adding 7,075.6 million metric tons per year to the atmosphere from our collective activities that use energy. The residential use component of that is estimated to be a whopping 2,720,529,000,000 pounds of CO_2 or equivalents going into the atmosphere every year. The U.S. population clock as of this writing lists the U.S. population as 303,515,783 residents, making the average domicile-related atmospheric carbon load per man, woman, or child equal to 8,963 pounds per person per year.

It's Time for Setting a Meaningful and Measurable Per-Household Goal for Carbon Emission Reductions

Scientifically then, when it comes to our living arrangements, reaching the least environmental impact can be easily quantified in terms of how much above or below the national average of 8,963 pounds per person your household contributes to greenhouse gases on an annual basis. An average family of four would have an allowance of 35,852 pounds, or 16.26 metric tons, per year to be considered average. If your current living arrangements are contributing more per person than the average amount of carbon emissions, consider your home to be the equivalent of a gas guzzler, or conversely a miser if consuming substantially less than the national per person average of nearly 9,000 pounds of CO_2 per year. Keep in mind that this is an economic issue, a social responsibility issue, and even a generational responsibility issue. You are paying the bill now for a rate of energy consumption, and in theory the next generation may very well be paying a portion of the cost of cleanup as well. It is hard to determine just exactly what form that future invoice for atmospheric cleanup might look like. The cost to future generations may go well beyond dollars and cents. It could come in the form of abridged lifestyles, a need to relocate in mass, or a giving up of some technological advances that have enhanced our lifestyles.

We don't always think of our homes or our living arrangements as part of the global warming problem, but they clearly can be directly linked to the issue. As we look toward a goal of reducing the impact of residential contributions to greenhouse gases, the idea would be to take steps immediately to reduce our own household's per person contribution to the problem. The goal would be to drive our consumption as far below the national per person average of 8,963 pounds as possible. Selecting and carrying out one or more of the projects in this book will help you reduce your household's carbon footprint. In addition, this text will help you estimate both savings in dollars and savings in carbon emissions.

A Long-Term View Is Needed for Evaluation of Energy-Saving Projects

As compared to European countries, the United States has few buildings, structures, or homes dated before the 1600s, which tends to shorten our collective view of the benefits and value of doing energy conservation projects as compared to European countries. In Germany, for example, there are buildings in use as homes that were constructed in the 1100s and earlier. In the past, the media frequently ran articles and features only about the energy conservation projects with a short payback period. This short-term focus, usually three to five years, is good for the bottom line of the energy companies and not very good for the planet in regard to the size of the carbon footprint that could have already been eliminated simply by looking at a longer payback term for calculating ROI (return on investment). The payback period should be measured in more than just dollars and cents and in a manner that also considers reducing the net contribution to the buildup of excess atmospheric carbon and CO_2 equivalents that pollute the upper atmosphere.

It Is Time to Stop Confusing Green with "Green"

There is enormous confusion out there about what it really means to be green. Call them urban or suburban myths if you like. Planting a tree, for example, is not going to solve the problem of greenhouse gases, even if everyone on the planet planted 1, 10, 100, or even 1,000 trees. It's not even the equivalent of putting a Band-Aid on the problem. Taking the time to recycle is often considered being green, but further scrutiny of some recycling efforts reveals they only serve to use more energy and increase the carbon footprint. Composting yard and organic waste is thought to be a contribution toward being green even though composting yields methane gas (a greenhouse gas and carbon equivalent). The amount of methane production from composting is thought to be insignificant. You be the judge; when the problem is calculated to be 32,161.8

million metric tons per year, can any amount of annual contribution truly be "insignificant"? In my view, if the air pollution stream, no matter how small, can be eliminated it is not insignificant; it should be a target for reduction if one is serious about reversing the trend of increasing levels of greenhouse gases. The only action that will make a significant difference in global warming is reducing, perhaps drastically reducing, our international consumption rate of carbon-based energy sources. The next time you see the word *green* in the context of environmental impact on the atmosphere, evaluate what is being presented as valid or not against the very real measure of how well the action, activity, or event will actually help reduce global warming.

So then what does being green really mean? The letters of the word GREEN offer up their own acronymic version defining the get-to-green goal. They stand for Getting Reduced Energy Expenditure Now! This book will introduce you to 10 projects you can do, now, yourself, to reduce greenhouse gases and save some real green money for yourself at the same time. Information in this text will allow you to calculate the difference these *green-my-home* improvement projects will make in your home, your pocketbook, and on the environment. You will learn how to calculate the savings not only in dollars and cents, but in carbon and equivalents not being sent into the atmosphere. Some of these projects will have immediate payback; others will require a longer term to reach a break-even point. In the daylight of a longer term view for ROI (return on investment), these projects have appeal beyond a single ownership of a home and look to the entire lifespan of the home or building. You may want to consider some of these longer-term projects as a legacy, in terms of fulfilling some degree of social and generational responsibility.

It is easy to infer that our taking responsibility now for reducing our dependence on carbon-based energy is being responsible to generations yet unborn.

Simply Focusing Resources on Being Clean Is Not Enough

Unfortunately, there is still confusion about what kinds of individual, corporate, and government responses will make a difference in reducing the overconsumption of energy and contribution of excessive amounts of greenhouse gas into the atmosphere. The term *green* is often applied—perhaps misapplied—to otherwise worthy projects and undertakings that have little to do with making substantial contributions to solving global warming, reducing your household carbon energy consumption, or reducing your total cost of energy. These often popular and frequently media-hyped projects are definitely worthwhile but should not be confused with ones that will actually make a difference in preventing the planet's average temperature rise from excessive greenhouse gases. Projects and activities touted as "green" will often appear in local media, such as when volunteers are sought to clean up debris and trash from a riverbank. A local factory may be getting good press reports for eliminating chemical waste streams or for capturing soot from its chimneys. Homeowners may feel good about using building products made from recycled sources, but unless they actually reduce carbon emissions, using recycled products does little more than make one feel good. Supporting government efforts to reintroduce an endangered species into a former habitat may make us feel good, and it makes for interesting TV viewing. Projects such as these are meaningful and demonstrate our collective sensitivity and our ability to interact reasonably with planet Earth. These projects are not necessarily strongly linked to our ability as humans to sustain our survival on Earth. Long-term human survival on a planet where the temperature rises above 107 degrees Fahrenheit is very much in doubt. What we don't yet know for certain is, is there some point when the Earth's temperature will spike drastically in a very short period of time from too much greenhouse gas? Will temperatures get totally beyond our ability to cope, at a pace so fast there is no time to react?

Projects, programs, and initiatives that do not directly reduce greenhouse gases fall into a category that is really more about the quality of life that is available in our environment. Essentially, these feel-good actions and projects simply make for a cleaner or more natural environment. CLEAN projects are those that Conserve (the) Land, Ecologies, Air, Environments, or Nature. Again, the word *clean* is its own acronym for the cause it represents. A critical reader will immediately note that the word *air* is included. Yes, it is included from the perspective of eliminating those particulates and elements of pollution that make their way into the atmosphere that do not contribute in any way to greenhouse gases and global warming. High levels of particulates can have the opposite effect by blocking sunlight that generates the added heat. It is a small but incredibly important distinction. Being environmentally responsible by participating in and promoting projects that simply clean or preserve the environment is a great way to be involved. Only the future will prove the greater long-term benefit of one form of green activism over the other. These ways of being green are not necessarily mutually exclusive, except in the sense of allocating scarce resources to one form or the other. Do we individually and collectively have sufficient cash resources to do both? If we are to err, the question is what side would you want the error to be on? Frankly stated: is it more important to stay clean until we cook—or is it a wiser choice not to be cooked and clean up later?

The amount of time, energy, and resources allocated to being green or "green" is set at all levels: individual, community, local government, nationally, and internationally. In two areas of our lives we are given opportunities to make a huge difference: in making decisions that affect our pocketbooks and in reducing the rate of consumption of carbon-based energy sources. Our choices for selecting modes of transportation are less within our control, based on what the marketplace is providing in terms of cars, trucks, or public transport options. In our homes and apartments, it is up to us to a great degree. The choices may be tough—install a backyard swimming pool or do a few projects to save on energy, cash, and carbon emissions—but they are ours to make.

Regardless of how the U.S. government chooses to deal with the Kyoto Protocol treaty for reduction of greenhouse gases, we as individual homeowners or apartment dwellers can make our own personal contributions to long-term reduction. The goal presented in the Kyoto talks as the U.S. share of the reduction is 7 percent. Reducing household energy use by 7 percent is doable without huge sacrifices to our lifestyles. A 7 percent reduction off the U.S. household average carbon footprint per person would require a decrease of carbon (or equivalents) emissions of only about 628 pounds per person.

Rarely are we as individuals given such an opportunity to quietly and independently take action to reduce or eliminate a problem with such a global scope and impact. We still have the freedom to make choices in our residential uses and expenditures of energy. We can choose independently of outside forces and be dependent only on our individual allocation of resources to make improvements in our homes or apartments that reduce domestic energy consumption.

Saving money by reducing carbon energy consumption is being fiscally responsible to yourself, your family, and your community. You are also being responsible to the next generations. Once an energy-saving project is completed, it has the added advantage of increasing its return from every future round of inflation in energy prices, as long as that domicile is in use by you or anyone else. It is reasonable to presuppose that price increases for energy sources such as natural gas will at least be in lockstep with inflation. Energy-saving projects are also socially responsible because your personal conservation measures reduce overall energy demand, keeping exaggerated price increases in check. This allows your neighbors here and abroad to gain economical access to energy-related consumption, contributing to equalizing opportunity and lifestyles here and around the globe.

As you read this book, you may have other questions about energy-saving opportunities or you may want to find more information that isn't included in this book. If you do, I invite you to visit the author's website associated with this book at *www.gettingreducedenergy expenditurenow.com.*

Green Home Living

Coping with Continuously Rising Energy Prices

As I began work on this book, I saw a public notice about a utility rate change in my local newspaper, stating the intention of my electric utility company to increase residential billing by about $14 per month for every customer using at least 750 kWh (kilowatt hours) per month. That same week, the television news included a presentation about the price of a barrel of crude oil reaching an all-time record high, even when adjusted for historical levels of inflation. Typically, when the evening news reports an increase in the price for one source of energy, it is followed soon afterward by increases in price for all other forms of energy. It is safe to conclude that readily usable forms of carbon energy are a finite resource and that with developing countries increasing their own appetite for fuels, the prices across all carbon-based energy sources will continue to rise. There are only two practical ways for households to react to increasingly high energy costs. The first is to conserve, to reduce the use of increasingly expensive carbon-based energy sources. The second is to shift away as much as possible from carbon-based energy sources altogether.

This text will introduce you to some do-it-yourself (DIY) projects that will get you started on doing both. Either of these alternatives serves to reduce your personal cost of energy, while reasonably reducing overall demand for carbon-based energy. It is a great win-win situation when you can save money and do your part to reduce carbon emissions into our shared global atmosphere at the same time.

Taking Personal Responsibility for Unnecessary Carbon Emissions into the Atmosphere

Whether you are a homeowner or apartment dweller, you can take steps to reduce your energy costs and reduce your household's total carbon footprint. What exactly is a carbon footprint and do we all have one? *Carbon footprint* is a relatively new term that has worked its way into the popular media in recent years. It refers to the amount of greenhouse gases (typically carbon dioxide) that is released into the atmosphere because of human activities that convert the energy stored in carbon-based energy sources—such as coal, oil, or natural gas—into the outputs we need—such as heating, cooling, and electricity to run lights and computers. We use (burn) this stored energy and convert it to other forms to do the things that are necessary to run our homes, factories, and transportation systems. In our homes we use this energy to cook, refrigerate, cool, heat, and clean dishes and clothes. These tasks necessary to run our households use energy and in so doing, contribute to increasing the amount of carbon dioxide in our atmosphere. Carbon footprint is the term that is used to define and measure the impact that human activity has on increasing the amount of greenhouse gases in the atmosphere.

We engage in many activities that use carbon-based energy, both inside and outside of our homes. Heating up a can of soup or making a pot of coffee will burn natural gas or use electric power that is produced from burning coal. A by-product of the heat that is generated is given off as carbon dioxide. Carbon dioxide, methane gas, and water vapor in the upper atmosphere work like a one-way glass or a one-way mirror, letting light energy from the sun pass through them to the Earth's surface. When heat generated from the sun tries to escape through the Earth's atmosphere, the presence of these gases in the upper atmosphere stops this heat from escaping, leading to a warming of the Earth's average temperature. This phenomenon is referred to as the *greenhouse effect*. The so-called greenhouse gases (carbon, methane, etc.) act just like the glass does in a greenhouse, letting sunlight in but trapping the heated air and radiation generated from that light within the walls of the greenhouse. The heat of the sun is similarly trapped inside the Earth's atmosphere when its upper atmosphere is densely filled with greenhouse gases.

Measuring Your Household's Atmospheric Environmental Impact

As we go about our daily activities and use energy, we contribute to global warming. Each time we run the dishwasher or turn on a light, we use energy. For many, just seeing the utility bills at the end of the month is enough to cause a wish for noticeable ways to conserve on energy expense. Some households, because of lifestyle or location, use larger amounts of energy for day-to-day living; others use much less. Many factors influence the size of our carbon footprint: home size, number of occupants, and energy efficiency. Where the home is located determines heating and cooling requirements. In order to save money and reduce the carbon footprint from our living arrangements, the goal should be to reduce overall household energy consumption per person to the lowest possible levels. As with all goals, a point of fair comparison is useful. The most logical benchmark for determining whether your current family living arrangement qualifies as green-home living is to determine how far below the national per-person average of 8,963 pounds of CO_2 and CO_2 equivalents your household contribution to the atmosphere is.

The Five Best Ways to Save on Household Energy Consumption

Downsizing

The focus of this book is on energy utilization in our households, so the question of downsizing has to be mentioned at the forefront of the discussion. Downsizing is surely not the most popular way to save on energy use. It carries negative connotations and implies giving up something we may not really want to give up, such as space for everyday living. Many environmental activists have advocated drastic reductions in our living standards in order to reduce demand for carbon-based energy across the transportation, manufacturing, and housing sectors. Buying a smaller car makes sense for some. Using less coal in steel or electricity production in our factories can make a difference. But keeping your thermostat at 58 degrees Fahrenheit in cold climates and at 80 in warm ones is not the right answer for most consumers. In order to take responsibility as one who believes that going green is the right thing to do, is it really necessary to move into a studio apartment or downsize to a home of 1,000 square feet or less? Some would say yes. And for some who are empty nesters or retiring, moving into smaller living spaces can often be the right answer. But in reality, if you move out of the old, large space, it does not typically go away. Someone moves in after you and occupies that same space with all of its inherent energy waste and inefficiencies. The net effect on overall energy consumption may go up, or worse yet an apartment may go vacant, while still consuming energy resources with no one there to benefit from the energy expenditure. Also, moving into an existing but smaller space does not mean that there is no energy waste within its walls either. The projects presented here make sense no matter the size of the living space. If you are downsizing by building a new home, these same energy-saving ideas can be incorporated into a new building, making for energy-efficient living spaces right from move-in day.

There are any number of other ways that you can downsize your domestic energy use short of moving into a smaller space. Some of them are very simple and require minimal cost or sacrifice. Washing dishes in a sink that fills with four gallons of hot water could easily be downsized to a dishpan that holds two gallons, cutting energy cost and water cost in half. Downsizing appliances or using smaller water loads in clothes washers are examples of what may work as simple adjustments toward a net downsizing on energy bills.

To find all the opportunities where downsizing something will help save money and energy, look at all of the places in your home where energy is used. Sometimes familiarity with the items we use every day makes us tend to take them for granted, and we rarely think of the implications of their use. For example, making coffee in a 12-cup pot when only one person in the house drinks coffee makes little sense when a 4-cup or single-cup coffee brewer is available.

Rightsizing

If you are embarking on building a new home, rightsizing that home to exactly match your needs is a viable option for maintaining a low rate of energy consumption. Smaller, more efficient spaces use less energy for heating, lighting, and cooling: the three major cost factors in a home's energy consumption. Opportunities for rightsizing also exist at every point where you are about to make a new purchase of anything that uses energy. The appliance salespeople are great at making you think you need the biggest one with the most bells and whistles. Rightsizing is all about assessing your needs and matching your purchases with your needs. Having a storage tank hot water heater that heats and stores 90 gallons of water all day long makes little sense when there are only one or two people in the household. So when you are faced with repairs or replacement of any energy-consuming device in the household, bear in mind that biggest is not always best. Try to match your true needs with exactly the right sizes of energy-consuming items you intend to purchase.

Eliminating Energy Waste

The first order of saving is to always seek out and eliminate any and all of the ways you are currently wasting carbon-based energy in your home. Doing so can save money on utility bills that currently provide you with zero value in return. There are so many ways that energy is wasted in the typical domicile, and some are more noticeable than others. People tend to notice the noise of a drippy faucet or maybe the cold draft from a poorly weather-stripped door frame. It is hard to notice that a home's attic may be underinsulated, wasting energy in both heating and cooling seasons. An energy self-audit can reveal many of the ways you are paying more in energy costs than necessary. Also, some utility companies offer an energy audit by taking infrared pictures of your home as the heating season begins, and others even have a professional visit to perform a more detailed energy audit. The infrared pictures reveal where heat is escaping from your home. Once you are provided with the information, you can take steps to make improvements in insulation, glass, weather stripping, and other areas that are unnecessarily leaking large quantities of heat.

Those same areas that waste heating energy in the winter are wasting cooling energy in the summer. The term *envelope* is used to describe the space boundary volume you are heating and/or cooling. If your home were a soccer ball, the skin of the ball is the envelope. For a temperature-controlled room, the envelope is the floor, walls, windows, and doors that enclose that room. Your goal should be to ensure that your home's exterior envelope is insulated and sealed and that air, heat, and cooling exchanges are done by design and are controlled or managed to your benefit at all times.

Seeking Maximum Efficiencies

Efficiency is a technical term with a very specific meaning that is quantified mathematically as a ratio. It means getting a job done, such as supplying heat, and getting the most output possible or value received from the input involved. It is expressed as a ratio of the output received from the input supplied, and thus it can never be more than one. It is frequently expressed as a percentage. The ratings on gas furnaces, for example, refer to their heating efficiency as a percentage of the heat, or BTU (British thermal unit, which equals the unit energy needed to heat one pound of water by one degree Fahrenheit under one atmosphere of pressure in a range from 32 to 212 degrees Fahrenheit). The rating is the BTUs available in the natural gas as compared to the BTUs from each unit of gas that is delivered into the heating system. A gas furnace that is 82 percent efficient is wasting 18 percent of the energy from the gas, presumably up the chimney. It is important to pay attention to the efficiency rating of all the energy consuming appliances, fixtures, or devices in your home when your goals are to maintain the lowest possible cost of operation, reduce carbon emissions, and save money.

Seeking Permanent Carbon Energy Reductions

The projects outlined in this book are focused mostly on seeking noticeable reductions in energy consumption by making permanent changes within the energy consuming or conserving systems in your home or apartment. Energy-saving changes can be in one of three categories. The first way of seeking permanent reductions in energy use involves mostly structural or system changes, which will create relative and permanent energy savings regardless of activities or lifestyles of those who live in the home or apartment now or in the future. The second way of achieving the reduction is to actively modify or manage the patterns of energy use. The third is to shift from a polluting source to a lesser or zero-carbon pollution source. It is of value to understand the distinctions because such knowledge factors into prioritizing projects.

Passive Reduction Measures. Installing additional wall or attic insulation is a prime example of a passive method of achieving long-term energy reductions. Another example is using six-inch wall cavities instead of four inch on any new addition. Both examples reduce long-term energy needs for heating and cooling regardless of the occupants' preference for thermometer settings. The present homeowners and future homeowners reap the benefits without having to do anything further.

Active Reduction Measures. Manually dialing back thermostats at night, for example, is an active reduction. Managing energy use with automated controls is an active measure or method of reduction. Active measures require some degree of ongoing action or attention to maintain the savings. Even something as simple as setback thermostats may require battery changes from time to time to maintain their performance.

Shifting to True Renewable Energy Sources. Wind, falling water, solar, ocean waves, and geothermal are true, fully renewable energy resources. The first four are fueled directly or indirectly by energy from the sun. Geothermal heat is thought to be fueled by radiogenic activity within the Earth's core. Geothermal cooling is made possible because there is a significant negative difference between summer outside air temperatures and the temperature of the soil at depths below 40 inches. Surface soil temperatures vary considerably and can be as high as 117 degrees in full summer sun and as low as below freezing after a period of winter chill. Temperatures at depths of four to six feet change very little across the seasons, and this natural reservoir can be used to collect or deposit heat.

Quantify Your Opportunities for Household Energy Reductions and Record a Baseline

First measure your household's current energy use. To get a feel for the potential for energy-cost savings from improvement projects, the best place to start is with your utility bills. Two years or more if you have them will usually give you enough information to establish a month-by-month baseline. If you are not one to save receipts and papers, most utility companies will provide you with copies of the last two years of use records for free or for a small fee. By examining the bills, you can collect and analyze month-by-month and year-to-year energy use for electricity, heating fuels, and household water consumption rates.

Understanding and Using Degree Days to Link Energy Use to Demand

There are two important comparisons you may want to make once you have collected the statistics for your kWh (kilowatt hours) of electric consumption and Ccf (100 cubic feet) of natural gas or other heating energy source, such as propane (usually measured in gallons) or heating oil. One of those comparisons is to the number of heating and/or cooling degree days for the period of time the heating or cooling energy was used. In order to compare heating and cooling consumption (and cost) to a standard, the term *degree day* was originated. Degree days come in two mutually exclusive modes, both of which share the same reference temperature. One heating degree day is a day in which the mean outside temperature is or was one degree below the reference temperature of 65 degrees Fahrenheit. For example, a day in which the high temperature hit 50 degrees and the low temperature reached 40 degrees would be a 20-degree-day heating day. The calculation is made by finding the mean for the day: the low temperature is added to the high and divided by two—(50 + 40) / 2 = 45—and the result is then subtracted from the reference of 65 degrees to yield a 20-degree-day heating requirement. Mean temperatures for days that are over 65 are similarly calculated, but the results are referred to as cooling degree days. To illustrate, if the high for a given day was 90 degrees and the low 70, the mean temperature would be 80 degrees. Subtracting the reference temperature of 65 from the day's mean temperature of 80 degrees yields 15 cooling degree days.

The premise is that on days where the mean temperature falls below 65 degrees, most houses require inputs of heat energy, and when temperatures are above 65 degrees, energy for cooling is similarly needed. A major premise underlying energy-efficient home design is to build a home that does not need heat inputs until the temperature is well below 65 degrees and does not need cooling energy until the temperatures reach much higher than 65 degrees. If a one-degree difference could yield only a 1.5 percent difference in energy costs, widening this temperature range by 10 degrees would save the homeowner 15 percent. Depending on the home and the area's climate, the savings could be as high as 5 percent per year for each degree not requiring additional energy inputs.

With an understanding of degree days, your utility bills can be compared against the heating and cooling requirement for your neighborhood's historical degree-day statistics. This comparison is particularly useful for tracking the energy-saving success of your projects. You can simply compare the energy actually used prior to doing an energy-saving project to the usage after the project is completed. To demonstrate how you would make the comparison, let's say that for January the total degree days for the month was 620. To keep the illustration simple, if each day's mean temperature was 45 (high + low / 2), each day would be 20 degree days. Multiply that by the 31 days in the month, and the result would be 620 degree days. If your furnace used up $310 worth of natural gas for January, your heating cost per degree day would be $0.50. After you complete an energy-saving project, you would make the same comparison using degree days as the equalizer to find the saving stream of the project. In the same manner, instead of comparing to dollars, you can use kWh, Ccf, or gallons of oil consumption (use) per degree day. By knowing the energy used per degree day, you are comparing apples to apples, as the cliché goes. In effect, you are making a fair comparison regardless of what the before-and-after project temperature was for the two periods you are comparing.

One of the best places to get climatology data for your town or a city near you is from the National Oceanic and Atmospheric Administration (NOAA) website at *www.cpc.ncep.noaa. gov/products/analysis_monitoring/cdus/degree_days*. At the bottom of the page is the link for the archives, labeled "1997–current."

By drilling down on the hot links on this website, you can get year-to-date and monthly totals of heating and cooling degree days for many cities in the United States. If your city is not listed, you can pick one with similar weather near you to get an approximation of degree days for your neighborhood. Local utility companies are also a source for degree-day data; just give yours a call to see if they track and publish the information. From now on you could also track heating and cooling degree days yourself, simply by recording the high and low temperatures right outside your house. Or you could use the weather reports in a chart, spreadsheet, or notebook and do the comparison from 65 degrees to the mean for the day.

Comparing Your Home's Lighting Costs to Hours of Darkness

The second comparison reference for expected energy consumption is for lighting only, and that is hours of available sunlight for your area. Lighting energy comparisons are harder to come by because it is rare for a home or apartment to have a separate electrical meter for collecting kWh statistics for lighting. Most houses and apartments would have to be wired with all lighting circuits split out on a separate main, which would have to be submetered on that main past the utility billing meter. Homes that are heated by natural gas or propane, that cook with gas, dry clothes with gas, and have gas refrigerators, are mostly paying electric bills for lighting, running electronic devices, or air-conditioning purposes. The current draw for the remaining clocks, smoke alarms, television, radio, and computer is usually small in comparison to the lighting loads. However, summer air conditioner usage will skew the bill for the months the air conditioners are running. The non-lighting electric load in a home that is mostly reliant on gas for heat and cooking energy would be estimated at 144 to 288 kWh per month, depending on usage factors for television or computing. To estimate your lighting load, you can subtract that from the kWh on your bill for the month's billing period.

One of the best sources to find out the sunrise and sunset times for your location in the United States is to visit the U.S. Navy's website at *aa.usno.navy.mil/data/docs/RS_OneYear.php*. Here you can select a state and enter a city, and the site will return the daily sunrise and sunset table for the entire year for that location. The sunrise and sunset table is useful for calculating the number of hours lighting is needed and the exact times. It is also useful when calculating the hours of potential solar energy available as the seasons change, both for passive heating and for solar electric generation panels.

If you subtract the number of hours and minutes of daylight from 24 hours, you will have an approximation of number of hours per day that the inside and outside areas of your home will require artificial lighting. The kWh used per day for lighting will increase when the amount of daylight is diminished by later sunrises and earlier sunsets. You should see a correlation between daylight hours and your electric bill. In North America it will decrease in the summer months from lighting needs being reduced by longer daylight hours. Of course, running the air conditioners in the summer causes the bill to rise anyway, but that can be quantified and compared on a degree-day cooling requirement basis. Many of the projects that can be done to reduce lighting costs will reduce the bill for every day of the year.

Getting Green While Maintaining Comfort and Convenience

Many environmental activists advocate drastic reductions in our lifestyles to be on the right side of the green discussion, while others still deny there is a problem. Regardless of which side you might take in the debate, it simply makes good economic sense to get a little cleaner and greener. Saving is good. What this going green energy conservation movement ought to be about is eliminating waste, maximizing efficiency, and transitioning to economically viable and practical non-carbon-based alternatives. Most people still want to reap the benefits of living a modern lifestyle, where use of energy enhances our lives for the better and gives us free time and energy to make contributions to our families and others, without having to haul drinking water or wash clothes at the river's edge. Becoming socially and environmentally responsible citizens should simply mean we are not energy gluttons using or worse, wasting more than our share of the energy pie. For lack of a better measure and to present a starting point for comparison, this text proposes that our share as United States citizens ought to be our per-person household national average. To be classified as green should mean a willingness to take measures to do our part to be a measurable amount below the current national average for energy consumption in relation to our family size, housing choice, and internal household choices for energy-consuming devices.

Making use of currently available and yet-to-be-discovered technology, not turning back to historic conditions, provides alternatives that allow us to be more efficient, less wasteful, and less dependent on carbon-based forms in our energy consumption patterns.

Being GREEN, as discussed in the introduction, in its truest form, is all about Getting to Reduced Energy Expenditure Now. In the next chapter, we will introduce some of the things to keep in mind as you plan for and evaluate your next green project.

2

Building the GREEN Project's Plan and Budget and Calculating Cash ROI

Setting Project Priorities

Deciding on which energy-saving projects to do at all and which ones to do first may sound like an easy proposition when the decision maker is sitting in an overstuffed easy chair reading about them. When faced with limited financial resources and getting up to actually do one or more of the projects, it may be easiest for a homeowner to opt for those projects with the largest return or the quickest cash savings. Some do-it-yourselfers might want to prioritize projects by degree of perceived difficulty and tackle the easy one or do the hard ones first. Other homeowners with limited budgets might prioritize based on the overall project cost and opt to do the least expensive first, and then use the savings afforded from the early projects to help fund the more expensive ones later on. What factors for project selection are most important to you is a personal decision. This chapter should help you with making that decision.

Project Planning

Some of the biggest challenges facing homeowners as they embark on do-it-yourself projects are getting the project planning and preparation under control and arriving at an all-inclusive project budget. Electricians, mechanical and plumbing, and remodeling professionals have an advantage when they show up on a new job site. For the pros some of the planning and purchasing is handled in bulk. They show up with a cube van or trailer full of all the pieces, parts, and products they are likely to need on any similar job. What a do-it-yourselfer considers a major project is typically just a routine job for the well-equipped and experienced pros. The homeowner usually has to make multiple trips to the big box or local building supply houses and hardware store for every nut or piece of pipe needed for each project. This is not very efficient, and all the while the transportation to and from the stores increases the carbon contribution to the atmosphere, unless you take your bicycle. The back and forth to the stores also adds to the total cost of the project.

Having a complete plan and parts list for the project before you begin is important for three reasons. The first involves accurately calculating the cost, which cannot be done very well without a completed list or bill of materials. The second reason is so that all the parts can be on-site before the project is started. Many people start projects in the evening and find that something is missing halfway into the project. Holding the project's completion over to the next day to run for parts is often very inconvenient for the DIY person and for the home's occupants. Finally, a good plan can assure that all the necessary coordination, tools, equipment, and person power will be available when they are needed.

One of the tricks for getting a good project plan together is a technique used in many professions and in the sports world. That trick is visualization. *Visualization* is simply imagining or daydreaming in your mind's eye, while doing the project tasks, step by step, one by one. First, place yourself at the actual project site with a pencil and notepad, then think through the entire project from start to finish. Imagine every step along the way to getting the project done. Write down each major step or task and list the pieces and parts, tools, and equipment needed for each task segment, and then add them up for the entire job. For example, if the project is to install new metal frame storm windows on the exterior of your two-story house, some of the steps will be: 1) put up ladders or scaffolding, 2) climb ladder to first window, 3) mark mounting holes, 4) drill pilot holes at marks, 5) lift each storm window frame into place, 6) secure storm window frame to window framing with screws and portable electric screwdriver, 7) insert storm window from inside, and so on. By visualizing each step and coming up with the items necessary to get the job done, actually doing the job later becomes easy. In this example the tools and equipment list will include ladders, safety ropes, hard hats, drill bits, drill, screwdrivers, level, marking pencil, tape rule, and drill pattern template. The parts list will include mounting screws, the storm window frames, and the window and screen panel inserts. To reach higher floors, the equipment list may include a rented bucket-boom truck, also known as a cherry picker, instead of just ladders. Visualization of the job step by step and making notes as you visualize helps immensely in planning and preparation for familiar jobs, and even more so for unfamiliar jobs.

Building the Project Budget

Over the next few pages, we will look at all of the factors that can significantly influence the cost of a project.

Buying, Borrowing, or Renting Tools and Equipment

Most apartment and home dwellers have a stash of tools hidden in a drawer or in a toolbox in a closet. If you are a new do-it-yourself handyperson or have never tackled sizeable projects before, you may need to do some upgrading and purchasing to fill up your toolbox for more involved energy-saving projects. One way to deal with buying new and necessary tools is to include them in the project budget. Then the tool purchase becomes a sunk cost and the tool is available for other projects in the future. This works well for basic hand tools and even some specialty tools where the cost is under some threshold, such as $50 or $100. When buying tools that you will use again and again, it makes sense to own them, as they will always be available in your toolbox. When the cost is higher than your comfort zone or when you know for certain the tool or piece of equipment will only be used once, you will want to either rent the equipment for the days or hours it is needed or consider subcontacting out that portion of the work to a professional (when highly specialized or heavy equipment is needed). A good example would be a cement saw for cutting in pipes. Cement saws are expensive and renting one would usually make more sense than buying one.

You do not always have to buy new; I have filled up many tool-boxes over the years by simply stopping for a few minutes and browsing at garage sales and rummage sales I happen by when doing errands on the weekends. When shopping this way, it helps to know what tools are worth, but you can often get tools for nickels on the dollar of value. Knowing what your tool cache is missing is also important.

Often, there will be the go-to guy in the neighborhood, who has the specialized tools or equipment you need and who does not mind lending them out to trustworthy neighbors from time to time. Be sure to return them, always say thanks, and budget for a tangible way to say thanks for borrowing a $400 nail gun over the weekend. The easiest way to do that is to give him a gift certificate from a popular nearby restaurant. Follow these steps, and the next time you need a chop saw for a few hours, chances are the good neighbor go-to guy (or gal) will be there for you.

Getting to know the manager at your local tool and equipment rental center can be helpful also. Often, they have experience with the equipment and can offer tips and suggestions for their use.

Include Safety Awareness as Part of Your Plan

When using any tool, particularly tools and heavier equipment you are not very familiar with, be sure to read and heed all the safety information. The six most important universal safety tips when using tools and power tools are: always wear safety glasses, wear steel-toed shoes, no loose clothing, use a dust mask with a HIPPA-approved filter, wear a hard hat, and never, ever get hands and fingers near the cutting blades, grinding wheels, or bits. The most important electrical safety tip is to always use a three-prong grounded outlet, or an extension cord plugged into or through an

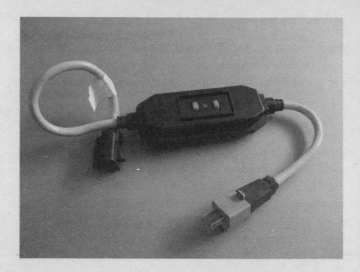

in-line GFCI outlet. (See above picture of an in-line GFIC cord. Keep one with your power tools.) When working on stepladders, avoid using the top few rungs, and get a bigger ladder whenever more reach is needed. Finally, remember that safety is as much about a state of mind as it is about having and using the safety equipment. Think things through, evaluate the risks of what could go wrong, and take steps to prevent it. Mainly remember to take your time; rushing can lead to a safety disaster. Include some money in your budget for safety equipment if you do not already have what you need.

Some Basic but Necessary Tools

Common Hand Tools. Ask any do-it-yourselfer, and you will hear that there are never enough tools in the DIY tool cache. If you are a new handyperson or DIYer, you might have to include some tool costs in your budget. Tackling any typical project requires, at a minimum, a set of common hand tools. Common household tools that should be included in a basic toolkit are the following:

- Pliers: combination
- Pliers: needle nose
- Pliers: diagonal cutting
- Screwdrivers: straight blade
- Screwdrivers: Phillips (sizes 0, 1, 2, and 3)
- Screwdrivers: Torx (sizes 8, 10, 15, 20, 25, 27, 30, 40)
- Locking pliers
- Channel lock pliers
- Wrecking bars
- Socket sets: metric sizes 4 to 13 mm
- Socket sets: S.A.E. sizes 5/32" to 1/2"
- Wrenches: open and box end 5/16" to 1"
- Hammers: claw, peen, and rubber
- Keyhole saw

Specialized Tools. Having the right tools makes any job go easier. The right tools vary from trade to trade and are often indispensable. Some jobs simply require having the correct tool, and any attempt to do the job without the right specialized tools is nearly impossible. These specialized tools vary by trade and include items like these:

- Circuit tester or multimeter

- Ground fault tester

- Tubing cutter

- Gasket surface grinder

Portable Power Tools. Many projects can be completed with hand tools. You can drill a hole with a brace and bit, but it goes so much easier with an electric or battery-powered drill. Projects should be fun and rewarding, and having the right power tools tends to make everything a bit easier and more fun. Remember how excited Tim "The Tool Man" Taylor and Al got on the TV show within a show *Home Improvement on Tool Time,* when using or even talking about power tools? A few that you might want to purchase if you don't already have them are the following:

- Drill

- Saws

- Jigsaw

- Skill saw

Rental Equipment. Rental equipment that might be necessary for your DIY project could range from a small item like a hammer drill to drill through concrete, to something as big as a motorized lift or bucket-boom truck. The best way to figure a cost for rental equipment is to first decide how many hours or days you will need the equipment, and then call for a quote. Some rental centers will deliver and pick up at your site for an additional fee.

Contract Labor and Professional Fees

You may want to contract a professional or just get some help with your project. You may need to contract a licensed professional, such as an electrician, to do some work that requires a license. When you hire a contractor, be sure to get the hourly rate or a firm, fixed-price quote before the work begins. Also ask to see verification that the contractor carries workers compensation insurance should an injury occur on your premises. Without the workers compensation insurance, you could become liable for necessary medical care. Such a surprise could be a budget buster for your project. The cliché "better safe than sorry" comes to mind; ask to see the policy or proof of insurance. In some historical and tightly regulated neighborhoods, there may be a requirement to get approval for projects that modify the appearance of the exterior of your home, such as adding solar collector panels. Call your local zoning official to check this out. If your changes have to go through a committee or zoning board, you may need a profession engineer or architect who is familiar with the process to help you get your project approved. Even with professionals it is OK to ask for a firm, fixed-price quote before you authorize any work. Most professionals will meet with you for a few minutes without charging a fee and consult about the engagement before you hire them for specific work.

Building or Remodeling Permits and Inspection Fees

In some zoning jurisdictions for some projects, such as with major electrical modifications, you may need to budget for a permit and/or final inspection fees. The best source to find out about permits and fees is your city, township, or county building official or zoning office. Some jurisdictions will carry this type of information on their website.

Labor

As a do-it-yourselfer, the labor component provided by you and family members is considered free. At this point you might say that at the office your time is worth a lot, and the opportunity cost of doing the project yourself is some huge dollar figure in lost time. The reality of it is that there is no substitute in the personal reward department for being able to say, "I am saving $xxx a month on my utility bills, and I did all the project work myself!" In some cases the free labor component is what puts a project in the positive ROI column from an affordability standpoint. A well-planned and completed project can also be great bonding time for the family members involved in the project. When you are getting help from others, do all you can to make the project fun and rewarding for everyone involved. Also, don't forget to get everyone on board with a safety briefing, and create a mindset to take time to be safe and do one's best work.

Expendables

The amount and cost of expendable materials should be estimated and included as a part of the project cost. Solder, sandpaper, electrical tape, pull twine, and drop cloths are a few examples of the expendable items that may not be noticeable or a visible part of the finished project or product. Putting them in the budget is important for accuracy in calculation of the project's total cost and also helps ensure they will be in your bag of tricks when they are needed.

Pieces, Parts, Fixtures, Fasteners, and Hard Goods

Do you recall the discussion about visualizing the project and the suggestion to make notes and build a complete as possible parts list? This list is referred to as the *bill of materials*. It is also your shopping list to take to Lowe's or Home Depot or your local hardware store. This list is priced out first with the estimated cost when considering the project, and then with the actual cost of purchasing all of these items to determine the final cost when the project is completed.

Information

You bought this book, and its cost should be the first thing in your budget, but remember to divide the cost by the number of projects you will do from the book. There may be other information costs depending on the energy-saving projects you decide to undertake. The zoning board may charge a fee for informational handouts, you may need to buy a book to learn in-depth how to design and build your own version of solar collectors, or you may need to purchase some manuals or catalogs. If it is associated with the project, its cost should be accounted for. This is basic cost accounting 101. If you include everything, there will be no "what abouts" (what about this or what about that) later.

Meals and Refreshments

No, soda pop and coffee are not really project costs, no matter how much of them you do or don't drink. A planned barbeque for the panel-raising crew might be a legitimate project cost. If it was really necessary to get the project done, you could make that argument. Check with your accountant or tax advisor whenever in doubt about attaching costs to your project for tax or reporting purposes.

Energy Credits

How are your wallet and checkbook looking, now that we are nearly to the end of building the project budget? If your checkbook is losing its zeros, you will like this part of the budget if it applies to your project. Federal, state, and local governments may currently be promoting and supporting energy-saving projects with tax credits, grants, or things like accelerated depreciation to encourage individuals and businesses to save on carbon-based energy or promote alternative forms of energy use. The nice thing about them if you can qualify is that credits are a subtraction from the hard out-of-pocket costs of doing the project. It is worth it to at least look into the topic and check with your jurisdictions for any direct or indirect subsidies.

Applying Costs

One final word about applying project costs to the budget. Any energy-saving project you undertake will likely cost some money. Sure, you can push the pencil about and move some of the costs around or spread them out over many projects. Some of the cost estimating is just that—estimating—and even expert cost accountants might not agree on the best methods and what should or should not be included. Just do the best you can to come up with your numbers for budget, and keep track of the final costs. Also, keep in mind there is a real cost in doing nothing. Unless you live in a dark, damp, cold cave, by taking a pass on doing any of the projects in this book or similar ones, you will pay a price for wasting your domicile's energy consumption. Your energy bills will be higher than they would be if you took action on one or more of these projects. Also, by taking a pass on doing some of the evaluation and homework to find your energy-waste stream, you will never know how much money is wasted up your chimney or is spent spinning your electric meter for no apparent reason.

Calculating and Evaluating Projected Savings

Over the next few pages, we will take a look at evaluating the savings and returns from the projects and learn how to compare the relative benefit or payback from doing one project over another.

The Two Most Popular Methods for Evaluating the Project Savings in Greenbacks (a.k.a. Cash)

Cash ROI (Return on Investment). When looking at environmentally friendly projects that have the potential to save money on energy expenses, a number of financial terms are used to rate or compare the value returned on the project expenditure. The most common term used is *ROI*, or *return on investment*. Simply stated, ROI is expressed as a percentage whereby the returning cash flow or savings is divided by the amount of money initially spent (investment) on the projects. ROI is a simple calculation but is only useful for comparison on projects with definable and known useful lives.

As an example, let's take one of the projects covered later in this text—installing an in-line electric water heater—and apply some numbers to calculate an ROI for it. The homeowner previously used a 40-gallon storage electric water heater with two 4,500-watt heating elements. Let us further presuppose a .92 efficiency for the old unit. Our make-believe homeowner lives in an area where electricity and taxes run 15 cents per kilowatt hour for separately metered electric hot water heaters. The homeowner is being billed $44.39 per month and is using 300 kWh of electricity in 30 days for heating domestic hot water. The new unit is an in-line electric tankless water heater with a unique power pressure sensitive switch that only applies electricity for heating water when one or more of the hot water taps is turned on. The homeowner estimates that 66 percent of the time, the old unit was heating water just to keep it hot, with no one using any water. The new unit's efficiency rating, because of the tankless design, is 98 percent efficient. The expected savings from using the new unit is calculated by first multiplying the total electricity used (300 kWh) by the amount actually used to heat water that is used by the occupants (34 percent), which yields 102 kWh.

Next to take into the calculation is the efficiency of the old unit (.92), which is multiplied by the previous result of 102 kWh to return 93.84 kWh, the net effective energy use. Dividing the 93.84 by the efficiency of the new unit (.98) means the new unit will only need to use 95.76 kWh per month to heat the same amount of usable domestic hot water. Applying the homeowner's current electric rates of 15 cents per kWh, his monthly bill after the conversion to the tankless water heater unit will be only $14.36 per month. If the new tankless unit and its installation cost $600, that investment cost becomes the denominator for the

ROI calculation. Here is where the time element or the expected useful life of the unit comes in. Tankless water heaters can last up to 20 years; for our calculation we will use 17 years, or 204 months. The estimated monthly savings is found by subtracting the cost of operating the new tankless unit ($14.36) from the cost of operating the old storage tank style unit ($44.39), yielding a difference of $30.03. Multiply this by the new unit's expected life of 204 months to show a life-cycle savings of $6,126.12. Using the formula for ROI, start out by dividing the return ($6,126.12) by the original investment cost for the tankless unit and installation of $600, which yields an ROI of 10.21 percent.

Other factors to consider are that the expected life of the storage tank unit might have been only 12 to 15 years, the cost of energy is likely to go up, and there is the time-value of money considerations that this calculation ignored. Opportunity cost, investment value, inflation, deflation, and other time-value of money factors are, at best, best guesses at what the future holds and should not be the primary decision factors for doing a project. As a side benefit, the homeowner would also get an endless supply of hot water from the tankless water-heating unit whenever needed, whereas the storage tank unit, when challenged, will eventually run out of hot water.

PBP (Payback Period). Another popular method of evaluating the cash return value of a project is the payback period. The *payback period* is a calculation of how long it will take for a particular project's cash investment to return its full value from the savings or cash flow received from doing the project. It is calculated by taking the amount invested and dividing it by the periodic cash flow or savings. If doing a particular energy-saving project leads to a monthly savings on a utility bill, the savings is the amount that is divided into the investment. The calculation will yield the number of months or years it takes to save an amount equal to the investment or original cost of the project.

As an example, if we take the numbers from the ROI example earlier in this chapter, the initial investment to install a tank-less in-line water heater was $600, and the projected estimated monthly savings was $30.03. To calculate the payback period, divide the investment of $600 by the periodic savings of $30.03. The result is 19.98, or rounding up, a 20-month payback period.

With ROI, knowing the useful life of the project is necessary; with PBP, the time frame necessary to recoup the investment cost is found.

Other Economic Return Valuation and Analysis Methods

There are other ways to compare the value returned from energy-saving projects that businesses may use when evaluating energy savings or investment projects. They may not be particularly valuable for the average homeowner but are worth mentioning.

One alternative to the two popular methods is NPV (net present value). NPV is a method where the future cash flows (savings) are calculated, and the cost of doing the project is subtracted from the total of the cash flows.

Another is the EVA (economic value added), which is a measure of the cash value of a project at the end of a time period minus the cash value of the project at the beginning of the time period. If one were to consider the valuation or potential selling price of one's home before doing the energy-savings projects, and compared that to the potential selling price after the projects are completed, EVA would be the right measure for evaluating the increase in capital or total investment value. For homeowners or apartment dwellers who stay in their homes, this is usually not a major concern when doing an energy-saving project. For those engaged in remodeling or flipping or turning houses as a business or major hobby, doing energy-saving projects will become as crucial to market appeal as creating curb appeal (appearance), modernizing kitchens, and updating bathrooms. It is a safe bet that home buyers will be willing to pay some premium on the purchase price of a home if it is green and as energy efficient as possible.

Another expression of payback on energy-saving projects is the rate of return (ROR). Using rate of return, you simply calculate the return or savings found as a result of the original cost or investment and compare the return to the cost on a periodic basis, expressing it as a percentage. If, for example, your electric bill was $110 before you took steps to reduce your lighting costs, and after the project was completed your bill dropped to $100 per month, your monthly savings would be $10. If the project cost $200 to do, the monthly savings of $10 is divided by the investment of $200, and the result is 5 percent ROR per month. In this example the project ROR is far greater than you could earn in a typical savings account or CD earning only 5 percent per year. It would be 12 times the rate of return of simply leaving the $200 in a savings account.

Examining the Added Value or Other Return on an Energy-Saving Project: the Savings in Your Carbon Footprint

Look closely at your energy bills for heating, cooling, lighting, cooking, water heating, and household chores. In some homes, well-water pumping, waste disposal pumping, and sump pumps also consume electricity or other fuels to do their work. In order to determine the amount of carbon emissions you can save, it is helpful to know how much carbon is expelled into the atmosphere before you undertake energy-saving projects.

Estimating Your Household's Potential for Carbon Savings

Getting to zero annual carbon emissions for any size household that wants to maintain any semblance of a modern lifestyle is not currently possible in the United States. In extreme climates it is particularly difficult to imagine a scenario where no carbon-based energy is consumed to heat, cool, or cook within our homes. I am not suggesting that getting to zero emissions should even be a realistic goal. After all, some carbon dioxide is needed to feed the trees in the forests around the world. Reducing carbon dioxide emissions should be important to you, if for no other reason than to reduce your household energy costs!

Earlier in the text it was suggested to collect your utility and energy bills for two years, if that was possible, to find your dollar costs and compare that energy usage to degree days of cooling or heating. The text also mentioned evaluating and comparing your electric use to the number of non-daylight hours. That collection of energy bills for the two years also provides the base information for estimating the amount of carbon emissions your home's current rate of consumption contributes. For these calculations your concern is not the dollar cost but the volume of energy or fuel consumed. From two or more years of the billings, you can see the trends and get an average for each month of the year. This is not about getting to exact numbers, but you do want to be reasonably close. Once you have figured out the totals and averages for a year's worth of consumption, you can multiply the amount of fuel consumed or energy used by an appropriate factor for that fuel or energy type, to approximate the amount of carbon emissions that you are directly or indirectly venting into the atmosphere.

Electricity Use. Electric energy consumption for homes or apartments is measured in kWh (kilowatt hours). To explain what a kilowatt is and to understand a kilowatt hour, let us use two examples. If you had a lightbulb powered by a five-volt battery and it drew two amps of electric current, the bulb would be a 10-watt bulb. If you hooked up 100 of the same bulbs to the battery, they would draw at an instantaneous rate of 1,000 watts ($10 \times 100 = 1,000$). If those same 100 bulbs were left connected and stayed lit up for one hour, you would have consumed one kilowatt hour of electric power. In the next example, if you had an electric tank water heater with two 4,500 watt heating elements, for a total of 9,000 watts of instantaneous draw across the electric meter, when this water heater keeps both heating elements on for one hour, it is using nine kWh of electrical energy. If you are running a lot of hot water and keep this water heater going for two hours, it would use 18 kWh, or twice as many. The formula for kWh is the draw rate in watts times hours, divided by 1,000. Your electric utility bill will show you the total number of kWh you used during the billing period, usually one month.

Carbon Emissions from Electric Power Generation and Use. Once you have the kWh, you can use that number to estimate the maximum amount of carbon emission that is vented off to produce that electricity. To estimate your carbon emissions contribution for electricity, use a maximum of two pounds of carbon emissions per kWh of electricity that is not used. The actual CO_2 per kWh will vary depending on the way your electricity is produced. Coal generation of electric power is pretty common and likely represents the worst case from a pollution perspective. Natural gas–fired electric power generation produces less carbon and may be as little as one pound per kWh. A household that pays 15 cents per kilowatt hour and consumes $110 worth of electricity per month has a carbon footprint from electric use alone reaching from 11,400 to as high as 17,600 pounds per year. Specific information on carbon emissions averages per kWh from electric power generation for your state can be found at *www.eia. doe.gov/oiaf/1605/ee-factors.html*. A small home with electricity to heat domestic water would likely consume about 700 to 800 kWh per month, on average.

Home Heating with Fuel Oil. There are homes all over the country that are heated by burning number 2 fuel oil. There are also too many instances where that same fuel oil heats the domestic water. For all practical purposes, fuel oil and diesel fuel are the same. Each time your tank is filled, you will get a bill showing the number of gallons it took to fill it. It is hard to know, for larger tanks, what month the fuel was used. The past two years' bills will at least give you annual totals. In some instances, careful review of the bills will show with some certainty the amount used over the heating season if the tank starts off full in the fall and ends with it being filled in the spring.

Carbon Emissions from Burning Common Heating Fuels. This calculation is easy. Simply take the total gallons of fuel oil and multiply it by 22.4 pounds of carbon emissions per gallon. There are homes in remote places that generate their own electric power with a diesel-powered generator. The same 22.4 pounds per gallon would be multiplied by the generator's fuel consumption to indicate the carbon footprint for making electric power on-site from a diesel-powered generator.

Heating and Cooking with LPG (Liquefied Petroleum Gas). LPG (a.k.a. propane) use is very common for cooking and heating in areas where natural gas piping is not in the infrastructure. It is measured per gallon and usually delivered by truck to an on-site storage tank a number of times per year. When the LPG supply company knows you're using the propane to heat your home and you are on an auto-fill arrangement, they use the local degree-day counts to determine when they should bring your next fill-up. LPG is also stored in 20-pound bottles and used in outdoor gas grills as an alternative to cooking with charcoal. The smaller bottles are typically filled on an exchange basis.

Carbon Emissions from Burning LPG. Burning each gallon of LPG causes the venting of 12.8 pounds of carbon emissions into the atmosphere. Cooking the New York strips on the grill, just like buying burgers at the fast-food takeaway, drives up carbon emissions. If you cook out and use up a full 20-pound tank, you will have used about 17 pounds of LPG and added about 217 pounds of carbon dioxide emissions to the atmosphere. A home's furnace that uses 600 gallons of LPG in a heating season will emit about 7,680 pounds of carbon into the air.

Home Heating with Natural Gas. In places where the utility company's infrastructure can deliver it through their piping systems, natural gas is often the heating fuel of choice in many homes. Some homes are even cooled by NG-powered internal combustion engines, which run the air conditioner compressor to provide cooling.

Carbon Emissions from Burning Natural Gas. Natural gas delivered through a pipeline is metered at the home's main delivery point. The metering and bill you receive typically measures natural gas in Ccf (100 cubic feet). When you look at the meter, there will be smaller values, but your bill will be based on a price for Ccf (100 cubic feet) or for Mcf (1,000 cubic feet). The cubic foot used for measuring natural gas assumes a cube full of natural gas (which is mostly methane) at a pressure of four ounces per square inch. When delivered to your gas meter, the pressure is much higher, and sometimes gas meters will require a correction factor to compensate for pressure and delivery temperature. Both propane and natural gas are promoted as clean fuels because of a nice, clear blue flame and their nondetectible smoke. Despite its clean reputation, natural gas contributes to carbon buildup in the atmosphere at the rate of 12 pounds per Ccf, or 120 pounds per 1,000 feet cubed. A home using an average of 194 Ccf per month for cooking, heating, and possibly cooling will spew 27,936 pounds of carbon dioxide into the atmosphere each year.

Unleaded Gasoline Electric Generation. Granted, it's a small percentage of homes—mostly remote farms, cabins, and lodges—that might use regular gasoline to make electric power. It is worth mentioning because even though a small percentage, it happens on a regular basis. Campers and RV drivers often bring along and use motor gas to make electric power while going back to nature. Even though it is not the main topic of this book, it is also interesting to look at your car's fuel consumption. Every gallon of unleaded gas use pushes out over 19.5 pounds of carbon per gallon of consumption. So just for fun, let's look at the numbers. If you're a commuter driving 80 miles each way, every weekday, 50 weeks each year, and your car gets 20 miles per gallon, the number is significant. The calculation looks like this: 160 miles / 20 MPG × 5 days × 50 weeks × 19.5 pounds = 39,000 pounds of carbon emissions per year. At the gas price as of this writing ($3.79 per gallon), it is also about $7,580 per year. We talked about budget and cars earlier in the introduction and how they are used for three years or so. Trading up on auto MPG (to say 36 or 40 MPG) can fund your home's energy improvements. Zero cash out of pocket and double your cash and carbon savings. It's a deal worth consideration. This may not work for everyone, but there is enough information here in the book to perform your own analysis. This book's price may be the best $7.95 you ever spent on getting green.

The carbon emissions factors (per gallon, Ccf, etc.) in this section were found on a U.S. Department of Energy website. To find these and other fuel emissions factors, visit the DOE page at *www.eia.doe.gov/oiaf/1605/coefficients.html*.

Setting Up Your Home's Carbon Savings Account

Use the carbon emission factors you found here, or visit the DOE website for other kinds of fuels. Use the actual billing measurements of use volume from your home or apartment electric, fuel, and utility bills to calculate your current rate of carbon emissions. Divide the total by the number of full-time residents to find the pounds per person per year of carbon emissions. Establish the total carbon emissions you come up with as your home's preproject baseline. After you complete one or more energy-saving projects, compare your energy consumption averages for each month of the year with the postproject, per-month consumption. See how soon and how close you can come to the Kyoto goal of 7 percent reduction. See how long it takes to get below the 9,000 pounds per year per household resident. Keep score. It's fun and helps you stay focused on turning greener and greener and saving more and more greenbacks, as you continue to complete the projects.

3

Fun Outdoor Projects
That Will Also Save Money

Finding ways to enjoy our time out of doors is probably built into our genetic makeup, handed down from our caveman ancestry. From the traditional backyard barbeque to the neighborhood lawn parties, cooking outside and enjoying our patios and backyards has been an American tradition for generations. Being outside also brings us closer to the sights and sounds of the natural world and all its wonders and increases our appreciation for undertaking energy-saving projects. Every now and then, you hear statistics about how much of our time we spend indoors. For most of us the answer is too much. For the people who track these things and turn it into news, they say 90 percent of our time is spent indoors. One hears a lot of excuses: I am allergic, it's too hot, it's too cold, I wanna watch TV, there are too many bugs, and on and on it goes. Some excuses are valid, and there is not much that can be done to remedy all of them. Some can be addressed with energy-saving projects that might even compete with the TV for the kids' attention. Some of these projects might make great father-and-son projects, mother-and-daughter projects, or help entertain grandpa on his next visit. Saving cash and carbon can be fun in more ways than one.

Saving Green While Enjoying the Green

Solar energy is free; free, free, free, forever free! It is safe in some respects from takeover by the energy conglomerates. We may have to pay something for the devices we use to capture energy from the sun, but the source itself is free, forever free. Anytime we can budget for and capture energy from the sun, we are not just cutting down on carbon emissions—we eliminate them altogether. This chapter includes some fun sun projects that range in cost from a few dollars to a few thousand.

Getting Away from the Smoke and Closer to the Mirrors, Thanks to the Sun

It is really easy to head out to the patio or deck and fire up the charcoal or propane grill without giving much thought to how much carbon is being given off by burning propane or briquettes to cook the brats. Every now and then, on days when you're not so rushed for time, this next project can be fun to do with the kids—and maybe it can even get them to cook for you from time to time.

Solar Cooking for Fun and Energy Savings. Instead of firing up the propane grill or smoky charcoals, plan and cook a meal around solar cooking. It is simple to make your own solar cooker, or you can buy a ready-made one via mail order for under $50 from companies like Edmond Scientific. When things aren't so hectic and you have time to plan ahead, you can both warm and cook food in a solar cooker. A well-made solar cooker can reach temperatures in the range of 350 to 450 degrees Fahrenheit, certainly enough heat to warm and thoroughly cook many foods. One of the easiest reflective materials to acquire for a solar cooker is a nonglass mirror, like the ones sold at building supply stores for adding to closet doors. Any shiny metal will work to reflect light from the sun to a surface. One choice for a surface material for a homebuilt solar cooker is fire brick. Fire brick has a ceramic content and is not as likely to crack from endless rounds of heating and cooling. A box of a half-dozen fire bricks can be purchased at many major hardware or building supply store for about $20. Spray the bricks black with a nonlead, heat resistant paint to help them absorb the direct and reflected light in your solar cooker. Put your cast iron cooking pot on the fire bricks, and focus the sunlight from pieces of your reflective mirror material on the pot. Use chimney brick for blocking the wind and keeping the heat contained. If you want to get really fancy, fabricate a metal framework to keep the "oven" and mirror above the ground.

Outdoor Solar Lighting Adds Safety and Security with Zero Carbon Emissions. Replacing 110-volt outdoor lighting with solar-powered fixtures will save money and energy. Typically, the only maintenance they need once installed is a periodic washing of the dust and dirt off the mini solar panels on the fixtures, to ensure maximum power collection from the sunlight striking the lamps.

Off-the-shelf, solar-powered fixtures work very well if the sidewalk and outdoor area you wish to light up has full sun for most of the day. If you are trying to light a north sidewalk or north elevation, the solar panels will usually not charge the onboard batteries sufficiently. To solve this problem, you can install a single large solar panel in an area that will receive sufficient sunlight. Next, connect the solar panel through a solar charge controller to a storage battery. Then wire underground from the storage battery to low voltage lighting fixtures. Once installed, the only maintenance is keeping the solar panel clean and changing lightbulbs when needed. Battery life will vary but it is not uncommon to get 8 to 10 years of service from a lead acid battery.

If your home is already equipped with transformer-powered, low-voltage outdoor lighting, you can consider eliminating the house current supply line and transformer and replacing them with the battery, solar panel, and charge controller setup.

Yard Divider/Wind Barrier. Some outdoor landscapers call this project a yard divider, others a wind barrier, but whatever you call it, when designed and constructed with a little insight it can be an energy saver and a way to increase the utility and use of a back or side yard. Conceptually, this project is about building a wall. A block wall, poured concrete wall, treated wood wall, or one of natural rock and mortar—it does not matter; the concept is the same. Think about Stonehenge for a minute—it was built to have a relationship with the stars and planets. Your yard divider, if designed and positioned to cooperate with the path of the sun, will extend the use of your yard and work to eliminate some of the too-cold or too-warm discomforts of being outside. I caught on to the benefits of a garden divider at a park in Ohio. It was late fall and cool, and I was there to look at fall flowering plants. A part of the garden was set off by a large stone and cement wall about 9 feet tall and about 20 feet long, with an open walkway in the middle. The wall ran mostly east and west along its length. On each side of the wall at ground level was patio stone, making up a floor area about 8 feet wide. The outside air temperature was in the low 40s. On the north side of the wall, the patio was 10 degrees colder than the air; being on the north side was like walking into a store cooler. Walking through to the south side of the wall, the temperature was noticeably warmer than the air, and it was quite comfortable to just sit for a moment and enjoy the sun's rays and soak up the heat stored in the dark patio stone. The beautiful thing about this type of project is that it can always keep you warm: during construction and every day you use it in spring, summer, and fall.

When designing and doing a divider/barrier project like this, the same standards apply as if you were building a building. Footing depths, structural strength, and wind load resistance all have to be met. Check with local building officials to see if you need permits and inspections.

Installing an Outdoor Roll Out Clothesline. Yes this is how your grandmother (or mother) dried clothes. It seems like a throwback to the dark ages. However, if you look at the upside, granny probably didn't need a membership at the gym either. If you can tolerate a little bit of exercise in exchange for zero-cost, zero-carbon footprint clothes drying, then installing a clothesline on a roller or pulleys is just the project for you. Even if you're in an area where this will only work for a few months out of the year, this method will save money every time you use it. Roll out lines are still available with mounting hardware, the line, and instructions, or you can fabricate your own with two pulleys, a clothesline, and a little bit of mounting hardware. Pay attention to load capacity and shear on all of the materials if building it yourself.

4

Harmonizing Your Home's Lighting to Improve Vision and Reduce Your Electric Bill

Right after high school, I joined the Navy as an IC electrician and later after service, helped out my older brothers, both master electricians running electrical contracting companies, on new home wiring projects. The homeowners and general contractors who hired us were concerned about two things: the project's surface quality and project cost. Very little concern or effort was put into lighting design. Builders were satisfied when we put in $4 light fixtures (a single one in each bedroom, except the master bedroom which might include some side lighting), a $20 fixture in the center of the room, and some would even spring for a dimmer switch for the master bedroom and the dining room. Standard home plans did little to address specific lighting needs. If you had to use just one word to describe the lighting in most new and existing homes, the word *meager* would come to mind.

Some, if not most, of you are living in a home where cost won out over good or even adequate lighting design. Have you ever heard the expression "what's done is done"? This old adage applies to electrical wiring and electrical fixtures in particular.

Once they are in place, it is rare to install new wiring runs and new lighting fixtures, rare to change them for improved function, and certainly rare to contract specifically for lighting design changes and improvements. I am not suggesting that you run out and hire for this service. The point is simply to have you recognize that what is there in your home or apartment for lighting—the layout, locations, intensity, controls, style, color rendition, bulb type, you name it—might not be right or optimal and on top of that, may be wasting energy and cash and causing more carbon pollution because of overall inefficiency. In case you missed it in chapter 2, every kilowatt hour could throw two pounds of carbon into the atmosphere. The sad part of all of that is that electricity is polluting the atmosphere at a cost of 7.5 cents per pound!

Saving on Lighting Energy while Maintaining Quality of Vision

This text does not propose to make you an expert on lighting, and perhaps an expert won't be needed for you to save some green cash on lighting costs. The proposition is simple. Take stock of what is there. Do your own evaluation of every room in your house or apartment as to the room's use and the "see-ability" of the lighting for that purpose. Here are some examples: If a daughter is into sewing and a room is dedicated to that hobby, can she see well enough to thread a needle with the lighting that is available? If you have a workbench in the garage or basement, can you see well enough there at night to follow a pencil mark with the jigsaw? Is it so dark over the kitchen stove that smoke can't be seen or detected until the smoke alarm goes off?

These are all lighting quality questions, and they tend to drive up electric bills, cause accidents, and frustrate the home's residents when lighting quality is not there. The lighting must meet the challenges of the room or subarea's intended use. This must also be true after you complete your energy-saving lighting projects.

Home lighting is for the benefit of the occupants and resident pets; it is also used to increase perceived security levels. The marketers of screw-in florescent lights might have you believe that just swapping these out for energy-saving bulbs is all you need to do. In some select cases that may be true, but in most homes a little bit of thought and design are called for to make some lighting changes.

When embarking on a path to save energy by making adjustments and improvements in a home's lighting, keep the big picture in mind. The overall goal of making changes is to save money and carbon without sacrificing "see-ability." You will want to have all the lighting function in harmony with the way you and your loved ones live in your abode. When a natural sound is in harmony with its environment it is most pleasing to the ear, just as when lighting is designed in harmony with its space and use it is pleasing to the eye. For light to be in harmony with its intended use, the elements of concern involve structure, intensity and control of intensity, hue, spatial relationships, and full agreement with the needs of the user. To be in harmony with the homeowner's budget, energy waste should be eliminated from the equation. Harmonizing with the planet means carbon emissions are minimized.

A Little Background on Lighting and Design Terms

Measuring Light Intensity. *Intensity* refers to the strength of the light, or brightness. Light intensity is measured in lumens, foot-candles, or lux. A *foot-candle* is the amount of light emanating from a single wick candle falling on an area equal to one square foot. Light energy output from a source is measured in lumens. *Lumen* has a definition designed to confuse the average reader, so I will try to simplify it. Stated in terms of watt energy per second, a lumen is 1/683 watts. A lumen is a measure of light energy per second emanating from a source. It is simply a way to compare the relative strength of different bulbs or light sources. The more lumens, the stronger or brighter the light. The amount of light reaching a surface is measured in foot-candles or lux. A foot-candle is equal to 10.76 lux. *Lux* simply defines the amount of light on a square meter rather than a square foot. The different terms used for measuring light energy are important because light energy is lost over distance in the same way a radio station signal is diminished over distance.

Distance Reduces Intensity. The level of light illumination falling on a surface from a single source lamp is reduced by the square of the distance from the source. One lux is one candlepower falling over one square meter of area at a distance of one meter. If the distance doubles to two meters, the lux drops to .25 lux. If measuring foot-candles, for one candlepower falling on one square foot at one foot distance, the illumination is one foot-candle. Increase the distance to two feet, and the foot-candle reading drops to .25 foot-candles due to the same light energy being spread over more surface area at greater distance.

Hue. *Hue, shade,* or *tint* are terms that refer to how the colors of things are perceived by the eye. When viewing the packaging for lightbulbs and florescent tubes, you will encounter descriptions on the box or in the catalog that relate to how that light source will impact your perception of the items you are looking at. You will see terms like *cool white, warm white,* or *full spectrum.* These terms refer to the effect they will have on the colors of things. Cool white lights will accent cool colors such as blue. Warm light will enhance reds and oranges. Full spectrum bulbs try to mimic natural sunlight as much as possible. These distinctions are important because simply shifting from a standard lightbulb to a cool white bulb might make reading the newspaper easier.

Types or Purposes of Electric Lighting

When it comes to supplying artificial or electric light, one size does not fit all circumstances. There are three general categories or types of lighting in your home. Each one presents distinctive opportunities for saving electric energy. Understanding these different categories will help you evaluate your home's overall lighting needs.

Ambient or General Lighting. *Ambient light* is the light that is just hanging around and splashing around in a space. Some ambient light enters a home by way of windows or skylights. It is that light that keeps you from tripping on the dog's toy or enables you to find your way down the hall. Evaluating and adjusting the ambient lighting in many places in your home will provide opportunities to save money and energy without a lot of effort. In a short hallway, for example, is a 100-watt lightbulb really needed, or did it wind up there because you didn't have any other size in the closet?

Task Lighting. Sewing, wood carving, and using your computer are activities that often require higher levels of light or light focused on a specific area. *Task lighting* concentrates a required amount of light on a contained area where specific activities, work, or hobbies take place. Task lighting includes a wide range of possibilities, such as a simple arc-necked reading lamp on one end of the sofa, all of the overhead lighting in a high school gym, or the built-in lamp over your dual-wheel grindstone. Task lighting should be sufficient in intensity and quality to support the human activity being done in the lighting zone.

Accent or Mood Lighting. Necessary or not, accent and mood lighting direct attention and create atmosphere. *Accent lighting* is the light in the case that displays your trophies or the light that amplifies a picture or piece of art in the entryway. *Mood lighting* is much the same as accent lighting in purpose, but more subtle. It is designed to give depth to space; it can create some shadows, leave some dark spots, and create a feeling. An all-electric fireplace is an increasingly popular home addition in mood lighting.

These lighting-type distinctions will help you to properly evaluate your property's entire lighting schedule, in order to find ways to save on electricity without being at cross purposes with the light's intended use. It may be possible, even probable, to save energy and at the same time enhance the perform-ance of your home's lighting system. I'll give you a simple example: imagine a bedroom hallway with a simple 10-watt lamp on a shelf so the path to the bathroom is lit at night. In this same hallway, there may be a framed picture of a Kentucky Derby–winning horse. You might consider mounting an accent fixture that uses a 5-watt MR-11 (small reflector bulb) over the framed picture that will highlight it and provide sufficient ambient light to walk down the hallway at night. Gaining two functions in one and halving the price for operation makes this solution a great trade-off. Upon examination, your home or apartment will likely yield similar energy-saving opportunities that provide enhanced value.

Electrical Energy (kWh) for Lighting Is Totally Wasted in at Least Three Ways

Lights On, Nobody Home. How many times have you come home and found no one there and way too many lights left on? How many times have you seen a neighbor's house lit up like a holiday party when you know they are gone or on vacation? This kind of situation is a total waste of energy. It is a controls problem, not necessarily a lighting design problem, which we will address further later in this book.

Oversupplied. Light can be supplied far in excess of what is necessary for the task or room's intended use. The choices for lighting levels are usually *on* or *off* at the switch. Excessively bright lighting profiles usually go unnoticed, as people rarely react negatively to modest or even large amounts of excess lighting, unless they are trying to get to sleep. Insufficient lighting or illumination is always noted, and complaints arise when it's too dark to see well.

Light Source (Fixture) Is Too Far from Observation Point. Light energy and illumination intensity drop off when a light is farther away from whatever a person is trying to see. When light levels are too low to provide adequate lighting, people often compensate by taking steps that waste energy: turning on extra lamps, turning lights on in adjacent rooms for the spillover effect, or by screwing in higher wattage bulbs.

Eliminate Waste and Increase Lighting Efficiency and Effectiveness

There are a litany of ways to save on your home lighting costs without sacrificing "see-ability" one bit. Television commercials and magazines are rife with ads for florescent bulbs that purport to provide the same light levels with less energy consumption. There is a difference in fluorescent lighting brought about by the fact that it is not a steady-state light. The fluorescent fixture flashes on and off with the speed of the supplied power, 60 cycles per second. This becomes evident when watching a motor turn or equipment such as a grindstone, which rotates at multiples of 60 revolutions per second. When illuminated under florescent lights, the rotating object will appear to be stationary. In shop areas, for safety reasons, the lighting should never be 100 percent florescent bulbs and fixtures. In contrast, an incandescent bulb heats a filament which gives off light, and even though the same 60-cycle current is applied to it, the light is steady because the filament cannot cool rapidly enough to stop emitting light for that mere fraction of a second. In shop areas always mix in some incandescent lightbulbs if you are using mostly fluorescents.

Lighting Inventory/Schedule. Begin your lighting evaluation by making a list on paper with nine columns. If you are using typing paper, turn it to landscape mode and make eight headings across the top of the page. You could also use a spreadsheet on your computer to make these entries.

Label the columns with these headings:

Before/After; Room; Fixture/Lamp; Wattage, Lumens; Task/Use; Distance; Dim, Right, or Bright; Switch/Dimmer; Type

Down the side of the page under the *Before/After* column, label every other line starting with *Before* on the first line, and *After* on the second line, all the way down the page.

Next, find every lightbulb and light fixture in your house or apartment and everywhere on your property. Identify and record the information for each light source on your entire property—every room and hallway, and including garages, workshops, the basement, and outdoor lights. A filled-in line would look like this:

Before: guest bedroom, ceiling center, 100 watts, 1,100 lumens, sleeping, 8 feet, bright, toggle, incandescent

The line for a lamp in the same room could look like this:

Before: guest bedroom, desk lamp, 100 watts, 1,100 lumens, sleeping, 1.5 feet, bright, pull chain, incandescent

The lighting use in your house will vary by the way you and your family live in it. You will want to perform the qualitative judgments column for all the lighting at night or at the times when the room is typically used for its intended task(s). When filling in the *Dim, Right, Bright* column, you are making a simplified, qualitative judgment about the quality of light related to the task the light is intended to accommodate. Using *Dim* as a qualifier simply means the light, in your opinion, is not adequate for the task, and you need more light to do the job. Using *Right* means that the light seems to be sufficient for the task without glare or hot spots. You really do not have to have a light meter to do this; simply taking the time to evaluate the light's quality at the right time of the day, keeping in mind what purpose the light source is there for, is all that is needed.

Find Maximum kWh for Lighting. Once you have your entire list completed for every bulb and florescent lamp on the entire property, total up the column for wattage to determine you maximum lighting load. This tells you how much electricity would be used to light up every light and lamp in your residence, not that this would ever happen. Once you have determined the total wattage, divide the number by 1,000. There are 1,000 watts in a kilowatt, so the result will be your maximum kW for lighting. As an example, if your lighting wattage total was 4,400, divide 4,400 by 1,000, which equals 4.4. If all of the lights in the example were left on for one hour, they would consume 4.4 kilowatt-hours (kWh). Each hour they were left on could be as much as 8.8 pounds of carbon going into the atmosphere at the power plant where the electricity is generated.

Take Steps to Reduce Your Electric Lighting Bill

Once you have completed the inventory and know the total wattage, it is time to take steps to reduce the electric energy consumption and if warranted and possible, make some improvements where they are needed in lighting levels. Every place where the list shows *Dim* or *Bright* becomes an easy place to improve quality and save. When the list shows the lighting is *Right* for the task, finding savings takes a little more effort.

Six Easy Ways to Save Watts and Kilowatts on Lighting

Reducing Wattage. A very simple way to reduce power consumption is simply to replace lights with lower-wattage ones. Replacing a 100-watt lightbulb with a 90-watt light will give you nearly as many lumens and save 10 percent on power consumption.

Switch to Lower-Wattage or Same-Wattage Full Spectrum Lights. Granted, this maneuver may not save energy, but in many applications on your list where you have noted *Dim*, you can obtain increased visual quality without increasing the power consumption.

Switch to CFL (Compact Fluorescent Lightbulb). When you take time to examine the outer packaging on CFLs, you will find that the lumens of output are higher per watt of energy input. The wattage can be as much as 75 percent less for getting about the same lumen output. CFLs come in a variety of styles to meet your needs. By using CFLs and paying attention to the lumen/watt trade-off, you can frequently upgrade the amount of light in *Dim* areas and still save on power consumption. GE and Sylvania both produce and market CLFs. CFLs also tend to last longer, needing fewer replacements.

Tone Down General Lighting Lumens and Watts, and Use More Lamps or Task Lighting.

Often, you can reduce ambient lighting and general lighting and switch to task lighting to make up the difference. Flexible-neck, full-spectrum floor and desk reading lamps are becoming very popular for this purpose. The light output is great and the wattage is low, and they can be positioned very close to your work without light glare, due to the flexible neck. Prices when they are on sale can range from as little as $20 to $70 and up. At $20 and when paying 15 cents per kWh, using task lighting can reduce net general lighting by 150 watts for four hours every day, and buying one could pay back its purchase price in 222 days. Another place that lighting levels can often be reduced is along pathways and walkways, but don't reduce them so much that hazards cannot be detected.

Switch from Floods to Spots or Vice Versa.

Spotlights tend to concentrate light in a smaller ray to focus light on a target. Floodlights, on the other hand, are intended to spread light out to a larger area. Make sure you are using the right style of flood or spot for the targeted lighting area. There is potential to save on wattage here, particularly if the application calls for spotlighting and you're using floodlighting.

Bring the Light Source closer to Point of Use.

All too often the solution deployed where light intensity is weak is to simply increase the lumens and the wattage. Before doing this consider modifying the location of the light source or moving the task closer to the light source. For close-in work, using a lamp placed at the correct height over the work area often solves the problem.

In some instances, using a closer source allows reduction in overhead lighting used for ambient light.

Be sure to enter the new lamp stats as you make changes in your sheet so you can calculate the cash and carbon savings impact of your lighting changes. As you make changes for each light source, record the changes on your lighting schedule and record the new wattage and lumens, and then reevaluate the quality. Try for reaching *Right* with every lighting situation in your home

What to Do with the Old Bulbs? One way to avoid tossing them is to use them in trouble lights in the garage or shift them to places where the light is only needed for short periods of time (like basements, porches, or closets). *Trouble lights* frequently get broken because of how they are used, so they are a good place to use up your energy-inefficient bulbs. Make sure to keep the protective covers intact so you won't have a mess when they do break.

Saving Watts with Better Controls and Switching

Not everyone will want to or can afford to set up a full-function, automated-controls system run by a computer in their home or apartment. Please, no despair; there are still some affordable changes and switching improvements you can make on a budget. You can still achieve better control over lighting cost just by changing from simple toggle switches to switches with some extra features. The choices discussed below are not appropriate for every situation, but you will likely find many areas in your home where simply changing how the light is controlled will save you cash and carbon.

Three Ways to Save Energy Using Improved Switching Options

Install Monitor (Lighted) Switches. Ever left a light on in the closet or the basement for a day or so when you were not there to use it? One way to take notice that lights behind closed doors are left on is to install a switch with an indicator light. A bright red light on the switch helps you notice that the light was left on and should be turned off. This will work when the neutral wire and hot wire are in the switch box. If the power leads (neutral and hot) from the fuse panel are brought to the light and the switch run is just two black wires with no neutral wire, a monitor switch will not work for that application without some rewiring.

Install Timer Switches. One good solution to ensure that lights for rarely used spaces are turned off is the simple job of replacing toggle switches with mechanical timer switches. Similar to a windup clock, the switch is rotated to the right to a certain number of minutes. When the time runs out, the lights are automatically turned off, saving hassle and money. Timer switches come in a variety of delay times and styles. There are also electronic timer switches available from Leviton that are available in programmable or preset models.

Use Passive Switches. Passive switches are those that do not require any action on the part of the occupant. They are marketed under the term *occupancy sensors*. When someone enters a room, the switch automatically senses the person's presence from movement, sound, or body heat and turns the lights in the room on. When the person leaves, it shuts them off. Some places where you would consider installing these sensors are bathrooms, laundry

rooms, and in the garage. They are available for three-way switching and can be easily exchanged for your toggle switches in most
applications. Leviton and other manufacturers offer a variety of
occupancy switches.

Combine some of the lighting options or alternatives in the previous sections to reduce your overall cost of lighting and begin
adding to your carbon and cash savings account.

Save Money and Energy by Weatherizing Windows, Skylights, and Doors

Regardless of the size or locations of the existing windows, doors, or skylights in your home, your first steps to save energy should not be to make wholesale changes to size or location. The payback on such projects may be very hard to find. Getting the most value out of the doors, windows, and skylights that you do have is the place to start. This chapter primarily covers finding and eliminating the waste or taking steps to improve the efficiency of your home or apartment windows and doors. One does not need to drive very far in the neighborhoods of the Midwest to find a home or a commercial building where large windows have been replaced with smaller ones, to the detriment of the building's design and appearance. Don't let a remodeling contractor take you down this path. There are enough product options out there today to replace windows and doors with any size energy-efficient models or component parts. In this section, let's consider some of the options you may find for improving your energy bill's bottom line without making a mess of the interior or exterior aesthetics or functionality of window openings or doors in your home.

First Let's Take a Look at Indoor Air Quality Considerations

Three design factors combine to establish the air quality inside a living space. When your windows and doors are closed to keep the house cool or warm, those three factors are controlled ventilation, spot ventilation, and what we will call renegade or unwanted ventilation. *Spot ventilation* is the exhaust fan above the stove that vents stove odors outside to let the neighbors know you're broiling steaks tonight. *Controlled ventilation* comes from air-to-air heat exchangers, found only in some homes, that constantly supply outside air to the inside of the home and exhaust an equal amount of indoor air outside. The heat exchanger does its best to capture the coolness in the indoor air in the summer and the heat in the winter and return some percentage of it to the living space, saving energy dollars.

There are two rules of thumb for controlled air exchange in living spaces. One (from ASHRAE—American Society of Heating, Refrigerating and Air-Conditioning Engineers) is to have 15 cubic feet of fresh air per minute per person. The other (from building codes) is for the number of air changes per hour, which is set at a target of .35 air changes per hour. If you live in a 1,000 square foot house, all on one floor, with eight- foot ceilings, the volume of air is 8,000 cubic feet. To change 35 percent of it every hour, you have to move 2,800 cubic feet in and out every hour. Divide by 60 to find that you must move about 46.6 cubic feet per minute with your ventilation fan to meet the code standard. If this amount of air is being moved in and out, it is to the benefit of the occupants. This does not necessarily take into account the ventilation needs of heaters and furnaces. Questions regarding indoor air quality should be addressed by a professional.

If your home is equipped with a heat exchanger, have a professional check out the air flow rate and match it to your family size. Doing so will potentially save money and add to indoor air quality. Make sure that the mechanical contractor is licensed in your state, and ask if he or his company is a member of any professional organizations. When hiring a professional HVAC designer, find one who is a member of ASHRAE. It would be nice if air-to-air heat exchanges had a setting for the number of occupants that could be adjusted by the homeowner as the occupancy changes or automatically as people come and go. The amount of energy savings potential from automating fresh air exchanges to variable occupancy loads is tremendous in homes and offices.

Maintain the Safety of Indoor Air by Constant Monitoring for CO (Carbon Monoxide, a Silent Killer)

The previous considerations involve air exchanges by design. Most older homes do not have an air-to-air heat exchanger, and even the ones that do still have other ways that air comes and goes out of the dwelling. If your home or apartment has a combustion-based heating system, gas stove, gas water heater, or anything in it that burns a fuel for light or heat, the most important piece of safety equipment your home can have, next to smoke alarms, is a carbon monoxide detector that is powered by house wiring with a battery backup. Carbon monoxide can kill you or a family member when combustion devices don't work properly or are not vented properly. Don't take a chance; if you don't have a carbon monoxide detector, get one and install it today.

There have been many newspaper accounts of how generators set outside the house to provide emergency electricity have harmed or killed a home's occupants. Protect yourself and your family; if you don't have a carbon monoxide detector get one. If you have one, follow the periodic test and/or maintenance procedures for it, and replace the battery as recommended.

Eliminate Energy Waste from Renegade Air Exchanges

OK, so you want to call them drafts or air leaks—that is descriptive enough. No matter the term, unwanted air infiltration or exchanges beyond what is required to maintain indoor air quality for the occupancy level is costing you heating and cooling dollars. The first step of energy conservation and cost savings should always begin with eliminating all waste. This chapter's projects are focused on getting rid of heating and cooling energy waste through stopping unnecessary warm air escape during the heating season and eliminating unwanted warm air infiltration during the cooling season.

First Inspect to Find Out Where Your Home Is Harboring Bad Drafts

Windows. Take a notepad with you and begin by examining every piece of window glass on the outside of your home. If there are cracked or broken pieces, replace them or have them replaced. Check the seam where the glass is fit into the window frame on every edge, and reglaze or reputty if there are breaks in the seal to the window frame. A small amount of caulking material can provide a temporary fix, but it's best to take the time to do this right so the repairs will last. Once all the glass has been checked out and noted or repaired, check out the fit of the window frame to its casement. There are many styles of windows, with categories such as whether the windows open or not. Each frame, regardless of style, has to be fitted into its casement to totally eliminate or at least minimize areas where unwanted air can enter your home. If there are broken pieces of wood letting in air, take steps to get the window replaced or repair the area yourself

Windows that open will have either really tight beveled fits or will rely on weather stripping of some kind to keep air exchange to an absolute minimum. Inspect the material at the joint to verify its full continuity on all four edges. Repair or replace any weather stripping that has seen better days. Typically, all you will need to do the job are a few hand tools. If your windows do not have weather stripping and are leaking large amounts of air at the joints, it is time to install some. I have been in a number of homes where the problem is a lack of or poorly maintained weather stripping, and the homeowner's solution was to tape a plastic film over the whole window casement at the window frame's trim molding. This works to stop drafts in the winter, but this certainly is not the preferred solution. It is really hard to open a window that is filmed over. It doesn't do much for the looks of the window either.

Skylights. Skylights have waxed popular for a time and then waned into a small niche in the marketplace, and then have come back in style all over again. There is debate over whether their benefit of letting in outside light (and air venting) is outweighed by their lack of R-factor at a point in the home where heated air tends to collect. Whether they are a good deal or not for energy conservation has a lot to do with your local climate and weather conditions. Skylights are also divided into ones that will open up to let in/out air and those that are intended to stay fixed and closed.

Doors. Everyone knows that leaving entry doors open and ajar brings in problems and lets out heat in winter and air-conditioned air in summer. Poorly weather-stripped doors do the same thing. Take the time to check out all of your entry doors to find missing or damaged weather-stripping material. Splice in new pieces where needed or replace the entire door seal if needed. Be careful when weather-stripping to make sure you are not creating a situation that makes the door hard to open or close. There is typically a narrow tolerance between the door and frame, and you should not put in too thick of a material. This is a situation where just right is exactly that—just right. Just enough weather stripping should be used to stop the draft without affecting the free operation of the door. Many times you will find the problem with leaks around door frames is caused by a sagging of the door, and sometimes a settling of the house. Problems like this may require the assistance of a remodeling contractor if tightening up the hinges does not solve the sag problem.

Another door problem that is not always noticed is a warping of the door from side to side, top to bottom, or a combination of both. Weather-stripping alone will not solve this problem; the door must be straightened or replaced. When replacing entry doors, consider seeking out doors with some insulation characteristics. The higher the R-value, the better insulation qualities it will have. Don't be confused by the U-factor, or U-value term. They are merely reciprocals of each other. *R–value* is the resistance to heat flow, and you want a high number. *U–value* is the ability to pass heat, and you want a small number. The number 1 is divided by the U-value to yield R-value. Be sure your choice of replacement door meets your security criterion and local building codes. There are strong steel entry doors available with R-values as high as 16.4.

Homes with solid doors lose heat through the door in addition to any air leaks around the door. A door has a lot of surface area, and solid doors become thermal bridges to the outside. Adding storm doors if you do not already have them is a good way to reduce heat loss at entry doors. Many newer designs are simple to add, and this can be done with a drill and a screwdriver. They come in combinations with glass and screen panels so the doors can be used to collect cool breezes into the house in the spring and fall.

Attic (Access) Stair Doors. These should be checked for air leaks and insulated. If your home's attic access door is not insulated, then look for a prepackaged attic door insulation kit; R-50 kits are available for improving the insulation quality of attic access doors. It takes less than two hours to install them and will save on heating and cooling costs.

Basement Doors. Basements sometime harbor spiders and other crawly things and are an avenue for unwanted drafts to enter the living spaces. Cool air from the air conditioner falls and can fall through your basement doorway into the basement to be wasted on the spiders and their dinner guests. Take the time to weather-strip your basement door(s). If your basement door or alternate leads to the outside, it should be high on the priority list for weather-stripping. Sure, your basement is going to be cooler, but leaks to the basement or crawl space below your home cost you money and carbon. Basement windows also deserve attention for keeping the home's total insulation envelope intact.

Meeting Energy-Saving Goals and Breathing Fresh Indoor Air Are Not Mutually Exclusive Goals

Older homes that are not designed and equipped with air-to-air heat exchangers or that do not have a fresh-air ventilation system connected as a part of the heating and cooling system rely on the fact that there are going to be drafts somewhere in the home to provide some fresh indoor air. If you followed the TV nightly news at all over the last few years, you might have concluded that the indoor air quality in many homes is found wanting. Meeting the codes or industry standards for indoor air changes is best done in a controlled way. Take steps to close up all the renegade drafts into your living space and bring in the fresh, tempered air by design. The solution you will want to consider is installing an air-to-air heat exchanger for controlled ventilation. In a typical install, the exhaust air is captured from the bathrooms and kitchen (moist areas) and the fresh air is piped into bedrooms and living rooms. Depending on the size of your home, you may need a professional to design your venting system, but doing the install is not out of the reach of an experienced or adventurous DIYer either.

Remember, with each of your energy-saving projects, capture the before and after energy use from your home's utility bills for your analysis and records.

6

Choosing and Using Glass for Optimum Energy Savings

While we are looking out the window to watch the seasons change or watch the kids at play, the amount of heat energy being exchanged with the outside air to make that view possible goes mostly unnoticed. A significant amount of energy is exchanged through the window glass. Glass exchanges heat at a rate that exceeds nearly all other building materials. You can take some steps to improve the rate of heat loss and get the same view for less money.

All Window Glass Is Not Created Equal

All common window glass has certain properties with respect to how it interacts with light from the sun. Visible light from the sun passes through the Earth's atmosphere with little difficulty. When the full visible light spectrum strikes clouds and moisture in the upper atmosphere, the result is a rainbow in the sky caused by the separation of the various frequencies or wavelengths of light. A rainbow with its full colors on display will render the familiar colors of red, orange, yellow, green, blue, indigo, and violet. When light waves collide with a surface (or molecules of materials, including water vapor) heat is emitted from the collision. The red is a longer wavelength (lower frequency), and the visible reds along with the infrareds are responsible for the majority of the heat that is generated. All the other colors and the ultraviolet account for the rest of the heating effect when sunlight strikes an object.

When light waves strike largely transparent surfaces, such as water vapor or glass, some of the light is reflected and does not penetrate through the surface. Blue light, for example, does not penetrate water vapor as well as red and the other colors. This causes the daytime sky to appear blue. The reflective property of glass sends some of the energy in the light waves back outside.

When you are trying to keep your house or apartment cool, the light's infiltration through window glass works against maintaining the cooler temperature. Using shades or blinds helps, but it also prevents you from getting the benefit of the natural light to aid vision.

During the heating season the reverse is true: you want the sunlight to enter your home and help reduce your consumption of heating fuels. Two properties of glass impact how it will perform in regard to passing or blocking the heating rays of the sun. The *translucent* property lets a given amount of sunlight in; the *reflective* property reflects some light back outside. Another property of glass affects how well it performs for retaining heat or cool—its ability to act as insulation. The density of glass and its thinness makes it, in comparison to other building components, a very poor insulation. Huge amounts of heat are lost through glass in nearly every home. The R-value for most single-pane window glass ranges at less than one.

How to Improve Energy Savings with Glass

Installing Storm Windows. The lowest-cost project that can help with minimizing heating and cooling bills is to install storm windows. Storm windows have been a common way to reduce energy loss out of windows dating back to the early 1900s. In the photo below, this older home has been fitted with easily removable storm windows. Simply adding storm windows doubles the R-value, drastically reducing the heat transfer through the window openings. If your home has storm windows, inspect

them and repair any loose glazing. And although it is not common on original installations, you can add weather stripping to your storm window installation to reduce unwanted air flow. If your home does not have storm windows, this is a good time to consider installing them. It is a fairly simple project if you choose from some of the preassembled metal frame models. Installing a metal framework-style storm window requires only a drill for pilot holes and a screwdriver. New storm windows can be found that have glass panels that slide up and window screens so windows can be opened for fresh air when the weather is nice.

Install Insulating Glass. Double-insulating glass is a presized and preassembled window glass "sandwich": two pieces fit into a metal framework so the glass panes do not quite touch each other, leaving an air space between the glass panes as a form of insulation. These air spaces can range from 3/16" up to 3/4" and as a general rule, the larger the air space, the larger the R-value.

Triple-insulating glass has three layers of glass with air spaces between all three panes. Spaces between panes on triple-insulating glass are typically 1/4" or 1/2". The R-value of triple-insulating glass will be three or more.

If your budget permits, you can consider installing insulating glass with additional properties. Manufacturers can increase the R-value of their insulating glass products by filling the cavity between the panes with argon gas or krypton. Another method is to suspend a film inside the glass panel to increase its overall energy performance. You will hear the term *low-E* or *low emissivity* applied to window glass products. Low-E glass has a metallic film or coating on the glass that reduces the amount of light passing through by about 10 percent. By combining these features in one product, window R-values of four and greater can be achieved.

Window glass is usually the biggest path for heat transmission (loss) in homes. Any improvements that reduce heat loss through glass will save heating dollars. Complete replacement of all of a home's windows is a fairly expensive project and sometimes beyond what many DIYers will want to take on.

Anytime a window is broken or in need of repair, replacement with insulating glass should be considered as a preferred option. If you are undertaking a window replacement project yourself, you can budget for and do one room at a time. Start your window replacement project with the rooms you spend the most time in. Your comfort will increase, and your heating and cooling bills will go down with each room completed.

Use Shades, Drapes, and Blinds

You can save some money by using close- and tight-fitted shades, drapes, and blinds on windows. They do keep the heat inside by modest amounts. For example, a single-pane window glass might have an R-value of .92. By adding a good drapery over the window, you might add as much as .4 to the R-value. If you are going for a certain look in window coverings, you would benefit from also considering the thermal properties of the material and style you choose to buy.

Watch for Variations in Window Frames

Readymade window frames vary quite a bit in their manufacture methods and design. If you are going to replace some windows with insulating glass windows, look for window frames that deeply recess the glass into the frame to reduce the effect of the thermal bridge created at the window edges. It's a small point but it does make a difference in the performance of the windows.

Save Cash and Carbon by Making Improvements to Your Heating System

The operational relationship between your home, its occupants' comfort, and your heating system involves many variables that impact the bottom line on your heating bill. Comfort level for a home's occupants depends on the heating system's ability to steadily maintain a desired temperature. The desired temperature can change over time and from room to room, or be dependent on the activities happening at a particular time. Comfort then is derived from being able to properly control the temperature. Overall, you want that comfort level to be achieved in the most efficient manner. There are a few projects in this chapter that will lead to better control and increase the efficiency of delivery.

Installing Automatic Setback Thermostats for Optimum Heating and Cooling Control

Some people are under the mistaken impression that it is more efficient to keep the heat (or cooling) on the comfort setting all the time "because it takes more energy to start it back up." Dialing back the temperature setting at night to more comfortable sleeping temperatures saves money and energy, as does dialing back on your heat settings during the day while you are at work.

The photo below shows a typical single stage Honeywell heating control thermostat. Notice the analog control dial and the integrated analog thermometer showing the temperature. If the outer cover were removed it would reveal the inner components, usually a mercury switch suspended on a heat-sensitive coil spring. When the temperature changes in the room, the coil spring tilts the mercury switch to turn on; when the desired temperature setting is reached the spring returns, tilting the mercury switch to turn off. The disadvantage of a manual, single-stage thermostat is that someone has to dial it back every

night. Dialing back on the way to work means the apartment will be cold when you get back home. Installing a multistage programmable thermostat solves these problems by allowing you to preset desired temperature settings for multiple time periods during the day. More advanced models allow for separate programs for weekdays or weekends, and the premium models allow for each day of the week to be programmed separately. If your home or apartment has central heating and cooling that is controlled from a single thermostat, it will have a summer and winter (heating and cooling) toggle on the thermostat. Most central furnace and air conditioner control circuits run on 24 volts. If your heating system is baseboard electric heating, it is controlled by a 120- or 240-volt circuit and will require a different high-voltage control programmable thermostat or a heating control relay.

Installing programmable thermostats is a relatively simple project for most do-it-yourselfers because the control wiring is already in place. The project usually only requires removal of the old single-stage thermostat, mounting the new one, connecting the two wires, and installing the battery, then setting the program periods by following the instructions included with the new thermostat to match your temperature needs. Start by programming for night and day temperatures to match your typical week. Some people set back the nighttime temperature to as low as 62 degrees. When setting the daytime temperature, allow some time before you get up in the morning for your heating system to recover some of the heat so you're comfortable right away. About 20 minutes is enough for hot air systems and double that for hot water heating systems.

Insulate and Tape Heating Pipes and Ducts

It is not uncommon for homes to have either hot water heating systems or warm air ducting that has no insulation. Heat is lost in the basement or crawl space and is not delivered to the living spaces. Sure, the basement needs some heat, but temperatures as low as 40 degrees can be tolerated there and will usually prevent freezing of pipes.

Hot Water Heating Pipes

Hot water pipes can be protected with electric heat tape that is sensitive to temperature and won't turn on unless it is needed. Insulation, usually fiberglass, can be applied to the overhead in basements to keep first-floor floors warmer.

Hardware stores usually have piping insulation that can be installed on hot water heating supply pipes. One option is tubular piping insulation made of a polyethylene foam material. They look like huge straws with slits down the side to make them easy to slip over the pipes. Another option is to use pipe wrap kits, made of fiberglass with a vapor shield or foil foam combination. Regardless of which method you use, you will want to tightly tape the insulation at the seams to keep it securely in place and to maintain its effectiveness. Taping also makes it easy to wipe clean any dust that might accumulate on the pipes.

Warm Air Ducts

Foil sandwich and fiber matting, such as those sold under the brand names Astro-Safe and Astro-Foil manufactured by Innovative

Energy Inc., are products that can be used to insulate warm air ducts. Your goal is to wrap the duct from the furnace right to the point of heat delivery. Insulating warm air ducts not only saves money, but it helps minimize or prevent a rush of cold air when the furnace cycles to on because the insulation helps keep the duct warm between cycles. This is another example of how taking steps to save energy impacts comfort in a positive way.

Replacing Furnaces with Geothermal Heat Pumps

Should you ever find yourself needing to replace a furnace in your home, do not replace it with the same type as before without doing some homework. You will want to replace it with the most efficient heating unit that will fit your budget. If your budget is in good shape and you have enough land for a ground source closed-loop heat pump installation, it will save you energy dollars for many years to come and will reduce reliance on carbon energy for heating and cooling. They will cost three to four times more than a furnace, running at about $8,000 or more. Your energy savings with a heat pump over conventional heating will range from 25 percent to 65 percent, depending on your local conditions for weather, soil heat, and the efficiency rating of the system. Three to 10 years is a rough ballpark for ROI on a heat pump system. If you expect to be in the same house for over five years, doing a proactive replacement of the conventional furnace with a geothermal heat pump may prove economical, as it will also add to the home's resale value. Energy-saving components will become the new "curb appeal" factor for selling homes. Home makeovers are slowly but certainly becoming green home makeovers.

Don't Become Penny-Wise and Pound-of-Carbon Foolish about Energy Alternatives

Having lived in the cool climes of the Midwest most of my life, I have experienced the need for heating fuel of one sort or another for six to nine months of the year. In my lifetime (do I have to tell how old I am to say lifetime?), I have watched energy use trends and lived through the changes where the latest and greatest fuel source selection was driven by price alone. Over the years our family lived in houses that were heated by wood, then coal, then stoker coal, fuel oil, propane, and finally natural gas. Now my neighbors burn wood again to save money on fuel, and I spot-heat certain rooms with electric fireplaces in the spring and fall.

All these changes over all these years (nearly 60) were simply driven by price changes, but notice they are all carbon-based energy sources. Sure, we may have enough coal and wood in America to last 300 years, but why would we want to? Shifting from one carbon-based fuel to another does little to solve the atmosphere's carbon accumulation. It would be amusing if not tragic if a company got TV coverage and kudos for burning waste oil to heat a factory. It makes more sense to move away from carbon to geothermal, supplemented by solar, and aided by wind energy. Wind generators, for example, could be connected directly to resistance baseboard heaters with a thermostat, which would send the electricity to the heaters when you were calling for heat and to batteries when your home was already warm. This is a simple but potentially effective supplement, so we can move away from burning carbon-based fuel. Regrettably, the marketplace is not keeping pace by offering simple plug-and-play products that homeowners would use if they were off-the-shelf items.

Whether you can take small steps to improve a home's heating efficiency or larger ones, every change adds savings to your bottom-line bill and prevents more carbon emissions. The insulation you install as a small project won't be wasted if you decide to change the furnace later.

Make these improvements and save some cash on heating your home, while we all wait for further advances in this arena.

8

Making Improvements to the Cooling System to Save Some Cool Cash

Cool Is Hard to Keep

Every object around us wants to take on the temperature of nearby objects. Your home wants to be the temperature of the ground it is attached to and the outside air that surrounds it. The sun, when shining, wants to use your home as a place to temporarily deposit the heat from its warming rays.

When outside air temperatures are steady at 65 degrees Fahrenheit, we typically have equilibrium and rarely would need to add cooling (or heating) within the home. When you do need to cool your living spaces consider the big picture. There are easy ways to save some cash and carbon, some that will last a lifetime.

Use a Systems Approach

By *systems approach* we mean to take a look at all of the things that can keep a home cool. The cooling system for your home is more than just the window air conditioner you install in an open window when temperatures climb above 80 degrees in the spring and summer. The home's insulation, the color of the roofing material, the color and reflectivity of the siding material, the attic ventilation, window glass (size, type, and locations), air flow, and home's materials are a few of the other major factors that make up the cooling "system" in every home. Adjustments in any one of these factors may influence just how much of an outside air temperature rise would lead to someone in the house wanting to turn on the air conditioner or central air. Modest increases in how high above 65 the air can get before you need to add cooling can save you a lot of cash and carbon. The reason is simple and is related to total cooling time. Picture two identical homes on the same block with the same elevations and exposures to the sun that are different enough that one needs cooling at outside temperatures of 70 degrees and the other doesn't need cooling until 78 degrees. Every morning that is between 70 and 78 degrees, the first home is already trading cash for cooling. Every night where temperatures stay above 78 degrees, the first home is using electricity for cooling 24 hours every day. Just by changing the temperature at which the air conditioner turns on can help you save considerably. In effect, it substantially alters the degree-day cooling demand factor. So let's look at some projects that may improve (increase) the number for your home's cooling demand temperature.

Ways to Stay Cool and Save Carbon

Plant Some Shade Trees

The most amusing thing that happens when it comes to add-on landscaping after a home is built is watching someone go to the greenhouse or nursery for some shade trees and return with twigs about knee high and as big around as a pencil. The temptation to buy saplings comes about because they are cheap. This is great if you are planting them for the benefit of your yet-unborn grandchildren. To shade windows, the exterior walls, and the outside play areas around your home from the heating effects of the sun's rays, buy some real shade trees—don't wait. You can use the dollar savings and carbon savings from real trees right now. For first-floor shade trees, buy a minimum of eight feet if planting close to a window and even taller if planting a greater distance away. For really large trees that will shade large areas right away, you will have to hire someone with a hydraulic tree spade mounted on a truck to dig the hole and transport the large tree from its growing habitat to your yard.

To get the benefit of the sun in the winter, select from tree varieties that lose their leaves in the winter. If in a southern climate, consider planting trees that will keep their foliage and stay green all year. Shading windows with trees is a double-edged sword and may not be the best alternative depending on the degree cooling days versus the degree heating days. The basic rule of thumb is to shade south (sun-facing) windows with trees if cooling degree days for the year outnumber heating degree days. If heating degree days outnumber cooling degree days, don't use trees, especially evergreens; use other alternatives to temporarily shade the south-facing windows in cold climates.

Consider Installing Window Awnings

Installing awnings, particularly movable (crank-down) awnings, can drastically limit the summer sun's heating rays from warming your home's floors and furnishings through the windows.

Awnings with a long reach out from the house will shade windows when the sun is at its higher points as it moves across the southern exposure of your home. The added benefit of using awnings is that you can still see out and you get the full benefit of the light through the window, adding to a room's ambient light. Usually enough light can enter to eliminate the need for electric lights or lamps during the day. With crank-up/down awnings you can get the sunlight to shine back into the house in winter.

Use Window Shades and Blinds

Installing window shades of the room-darkening or light-diffusing variety can be an inexpensive method to reflect some of the sunlight back outside and keep the room cooler. It makes you wonder why no one has made a blind with reflective white on one side and absorbing black on the other with a mode on the mechanism to switch them over from season to season or day to day. Too complicated I guess. In any case shades and blinds can help, and their cost and degree of difficulty to install is minimal.

Install Powered Attic Ventilation

For homes with attics, adding a powered ventilator to run the sun's heat from the roof outside is a great way to reduce the use of the air conditioner. Once the attic is heated from the sun on the roof, it heats the insulation on the attic floor, and finally the drywall ceiling temperature is raised from the heat on both sides. When the ceiling temperature is raised in this way, it is no longer a path for heat loss. The natural air flow ventilation built into a home is often inadequate to cool the attic space enough. The air conditioner inside your home will have to work harder if the attic temperatures are warm enough to bleed heat through the thermal bridge of the ceiling into the living spaces. By installing a powered attic ventilation fan and controlling it with a thermostat, you can help keep your home cooler and reduce the length of time the air conditioner has to run. Even though the attic vent fan will be on, it uses less electricity than the air-conditioning compressor and fans.

Cooling Pipe

A very primitive way to take advantage of the Earth's cooler temperature without installing a full heat pump system for cooling is to bury a 6-inch continuous pipe loop in the ground at about 40 inches deep or so. Then pull hot air off of a room's ceiling with a thermostatically controlled fan to blow that air into the buried pipe. At the return point of the loop, vent the now cooled air out onto the floor of the room. A very small vent booster fan can be used to move the air through the pipe. Because you need 600 feet of pipe in the buried loop to make it worthwhile, a project like this is not for everyone. The upside is there is only one moving part, and it can benefit the home's occupants forever theoretically.

Use Point-of-Delivery Air Conditioners

Adding a point-of-delivery air conditioner is a great way to cool one to three rooms. They are also called ductless air conditioners because there are no air ducts, like in central air systems. It even makes sense to install them in homes that already have central air-conditioning, particularly in larger homes of 2,500 square feet or more, anywhere the central air-conditioning is not zoned and controlled with separate thermostats. These are not window-mounted portable units; they are full-blown air conditioners, and they have an outdoor condenser and an indoor evaporator just like central air units—however with central air, you only have one evaporator and one condenser. With a point-of-delivery system, you can also have a one-to-one relationship if you are just intending to cool one room. If you want to cool more rooms with a point-of-delivery air system, you still only have one outdoor condenser, but you can have one, two, three, or four (sometimes called single, dual, tri, and quad) indoor evaporators each in a different room. Each room unit can have its own thermostat and convenient remote control for setting the temperature.

Installation only requires a three-inch or four-inch round hole from the inside to the outside to run the coolant lines and control wiring to the unit outside. Depending on the manufacturer, the lines can be run for up to 50 feet from the outdoor unit.

The reasons why ductless units can be net energy savers begins with the waste involved in central air systems. First of all, cooling losses from a central air system through the ducts can reach 25 to 30 percent. Home central air systems are not usually zoned. The heating ducts usually double as air-conditioning ducts and are designed to bring heat to every room. When a single evaporator sits on top (or bottom) of the furnace feeding into the vent pipe, there is only one thermostat for setting the temperature in the whole house. As a result, some rooms are overcooled and others are not cool enough. With a ductless air-conditioning system installed in frequently used rooms, you can cool only the spaces where you spend the most time.

Take care to get a ductless system that is the right size for the room's needs; too small or too large a unit can also waste energy. Have a licensed mechanical contractor size and install the unit(s), or consult with a professional to help you get the right sizes for the rooms you need to cool.

Install Automated, Programmable Controls for Cooling, Too

Let rooms stay warm when not in use and cool only when needed. There is no reason to keep the house at 60 degrees in the hot summer months if everyone is away at school or work during the hottest part of the day. The argument that it takes more energy to cool things back down is simply not true, just like there is no justification for leaving a light on in a room when the room is vacated for a few minutes. Off is off; off equals zero energy consumption for the time a light, furnace, or air conditioner is off. If your system is sized correctly, programming the air back to the desired temperature one hour before the first person arrives should be sufficient. In the average day, you would get a seven- or eight-to-one rate of savings by using programmable controls. Concern about pets is valid and is another reason to consider installing the ductless air conditioners. Fido or Puff Muffin will be smart enough to find and stay in the one cool room!

Seeking Cooling Efficiency

Eliminate Bleed Off of Cooling Capacity

Just as heat ducts perform best when insulated to their point of delivery, the same is true with cooling ducts. In many homes that use a hot air system, the heating ducts and hot air ducts are the same ducts and use the same air delivery fans. If you have a separate ducted cooling system and/or you have not already insulated your cooling/heating ducts, doing so can save you money by delivering more of the cooling to the areas you want to cool. Wrap appropriate insulating material around all sides of the duct and tightly tape all of the seams to reduce air and moisture infiltration to and from the duct. See chapter 7 for more information on heating duct insulation.

Changing Colors Can Help

When repainting or re-siding your house or replacing roof shingles, consider changing to colors that follow these simple rules: If degree heating days where you live outnumber degree cooling days, migrate to dark, sunlight-absorbing colors. If cooling degree days outnumber heating degree days, drift your color scheme choices toward white colors and more sunlight-reflective materials.

Pay Attention to Unit Efficiency

The efficiency rating of any central, point, or portable air conditioner should be at the top of you criteria list for comparing cooling equipment of any kind. The efficiency rating applies directly to the dollar cost of operation. Think of it this way: If you have a dollar's worth of cooling demand, an air conditioner that is .92 efficient will cost you $1.08 to do the job. Another unit with a .87 efficiency will cost you $1.15 to get the job done. Simply divide one by the efficiency to make these comparisons easy. The same is true of carbon savings—two pounds of carbon at unity—2.17 pounds at .92, and 2.30 at .87; the rating works either way.

Keeping your cool and keeping more of your cash by doing one or more of these projects will impact your electric bill in a positive way. Remember to record the before- and after-project energy consumption.

9

Reduce Your Electric Bill by Installing Reduced-Energy Appliances and Fixtures

Lesson from History

If you are old enough you might remember the toasters with the red-hot wire coils inside and the two flop-down sides where you put the bread. If you were not careful, a few seconds too long in that appliance and your toast went from nicely browned to totally black and burned. Even the chickens wouldn't eat that toast—carbon and charcoal from what used to be a nice fresh piece of home-baked bread. Energy was cheap then by comparison, so these and many other appliances were overpowered to get the job done. They might have even worked in a brownout, better perhaps with a little less electricity supplied to them. Toasters and indeed almost every appliance you would buy today are far more energy efficient. Manufacturers have found many ways to apply the principles of good design and have attained just the right balance between power and control. The lesson from history is that this idea of getting to reduced energy use in home products is a moving target. Up to the point of the limits and laws of the physical world, you can always squeeze a little more efficiency and performance. The good news is that in a lot of products there is still much room for improvement. We will eventually hit a wall when it comes to carbon savings, once all products reach the physical limitations of natural laws and there is no more efficiency to achieve. At that point, shifting entirely away from carbon forms and sources of energy will have to be the only remaining priority. The older the appliance or product you are replacing, the higher the probability there are much better ones out there from an energy-use standpoint. The U.S. government has even set up a website to help you find them.

An Easy Way to Reduce Energy Use

Apart from lightbulb replacement, installing reduced-energy appliances is perhaps the easiest project to undertake to save on your utility bills and reduce your household's carbon footprint. You simply bring the smaller items home new from the store and plug them in to replace the old ones. You can usually get the store to deliver and hook up larger appliances for you, and they will haul away the old ones.

The U.S. government-sponsored Energy Star program began in the early 1990s as a voluntary labeling program of the U.S. Environmental Protection Agency. Its intent was to help consumers find energy-efficient products that would save them money on their utility bills and at the same time reduce contributions to greenhouse gas emissions. The program has grown to include the U.S. Department of Energy, and now the label can be found on 50 energy-consuming product categories. Getting a product on this list requires that it be more efficient than other models currently manufactured. There are differences across product lines from many manufacturers, so you still have to research and shop around to find the best products for your budget and situation.

More energy efficient items that can be found in the current marketplace include the following:

- Battery chargers

- Clothes washers

- Dehumidifiers

- Refrigerators

- Room air conditioners

- Furnaces

- Central air systems

- Heat pumps

- Televisions

Estimating the Savings

The labeling program includes annual energy consumption estimates for the appliances. You can use the numbers for kWh consumption on the labels and multiply by your cost of electricity to get a closer estimate of the cost of operation of one product over another. One way to get a rough estimate of the savings is to read the wattage label on your old appliance and compare to the wattage label on the new appliance. It's a very rough comparison because controls and run times will make a lot of difference as well.

To find out more about furnaces, appliances, and home electronics, along with other topics of energy interest to consumers, visit the U.S. government's energy website at *www.energystar.gov*. See if you can find the label that means the product or appliance has met the energy-efficiency criteria.

Capturing Electrical Energy from Sunlight

There are five sources of energy which are considered to be nonpolluting and the energy in them can be fairly easily converted into electrical power or heat energy. Solar, wind, falling water (essentially rain), tides, and geothermal are the least polluting forms of energy. In this chapter we will examine ways to collect energy from the sun and convert it to usable electric power.

Solar Electric Power Basics

In order to understand the benefits of taking on the projects in this section and how they work, it is necessary to understand a little about the physics of electricity. If you already understand basic electricity you might want to skip this section.

Electricity, whether it comes from a battery, a lightning storm, or the utility company serving your neighborhood, is simply the movement of electrons through materials that can conduct them. *Conduct* means to accommodate the movement of electrons from one place to another. An atom is the smallest unit of uniform matter that is either a solid, gas, liquid, or plasma. Electrons are on the outer ring of atoms, and when these tiny particles move from one atom to another that is electrical power. Bolts of lightning that you see in a summer storm are electrons moving through the air.

Electricity can be made from sunlight when the energy in the sunlight's rays causes an electron in a material to move from one atom to another. Electric solar cells take advantage of those moving electrons by using dissimilar materials—one material with electrons that can be easily shaken loose from their atoms and another material that wants to collect electrons. These dissimilar materials form the positive and negative plates of solar electric cells. Installing many of these cells on a panel and having a lot of surface area increases the electrical pressure and quantity of electrons collected in the panel. When struck by sunlight, the panel produces DC (direct current) electrical power, like a battery in a flashlight.

Long Sunny Days Produce the Most Solar Electric Power

Weather conditions in your area will play a major role in the effectiveness of any attempt to capture energy from the sun and convert it to heat or electrical power. Cloudy days and length of daylight affect the amount of electric power you can get from solar electric panels. They produce power best on a bright, sunny day when their flat surface is angled to be perpendicular to the path of the sun. As the year and seasons progress, the sun's arc across the sky changes. The sun's path from sunrise to sunset is wider and higher in the summer and narrower and lower in the winter.

Two Ways to Harness Solar Electric Power

Electrical energy from the sun can be used as soon as it is produced—by powering something directly or by routing it to a bank of storage batteries for later use.

Solar arrays connected to batteries are designed to meet a constant 24-hour kWh load. To do so the solar panels must be sized to collect enough electric power and store it even on the short light days.

Sharing Your Homegrown Electric Power with the Grid

Your house, when connected to the electrical grid, is connected to what seems to be an unlimited reservoir or limitless supply of electricity. During the day the rate of electric power use in your house changes from a low to a high rate of consumption. One application of home solar electric power generation that is gaining popularity is to deploy a solar array with an electronic controller connected to your home's electric load and by default to the power grid. The electronic control, to satisfy the safety concerns of the utility companies, shuts your power generation system off from the grid when the grid's power goes out. The home solar power generation in these applications does not need a bank of batteries. The operation and power production follows the cycles of the sun and begins to produce power when the sun comes up. The electric load in your house is assisted by this, as it has combined sources of power. As people leave for work and the electric load is reduced because appliances and electronics are turned off, there comes a point when all of the home's electricity needs are supplied by the solar energy system. After a time the home's load drops and the sun's input to the solar array increases and begins to turn your electric meter backward, building you credits on your electric bill. As people return home, the load increases and you run for a time with both the grid and your system supplying power. As the sun recedes on the horizon, the home power generation system stops producing power, and you are again supplied completely from the grid for your electric power needs. The next day the cycle repeats.

The above scenario works because the electricity itself and the electronic controls operate like a pressure switch, always moving the electricity to the greatest need or heaviest load. Imagine two tanks full of water with a hose connecting them at the bottom of the tanks. The tank that is fullest will share its water with the tank that needs it. Increase the water in the opposite tank, and water flows the other way. In this picture the hose is the electric meter, measuring flow from one tank to the other.

The components for a direct connect system are the control/inverter combination and the solar arrays that connect to the control. The advantage is that it is a simple system and does not require maintenance or periodic replacement of batteries.

State and Local Laws and Codes Regulating Your Connection to Electric Utilities

Utility companies are not very excited about you making your own electrical power. It has been a struggle for the solar panel pioneers running their own electrical generating plants to get permission from the electrical companies to hook up and make money by supplying electrical power to the grid. As a result of their persistence and the power companies' collective resistance, many states have passed *net metering* regulations, requiring the power companies to let you connect and push electricity backward through your electric meter into the grid.

To find out more about net metering in your state and other alternative energy policies and information, visit this website: *www.dsireusa.org*. There is a state-by-state map with hot links to more information. For an informative article on the DOE website, visit this Web page and click on some of the links to learn more: *www.eere.energy.gov/states/alternatives/net_metering.cfm*.

Start Small and Grow Your Solar Electric Power Plant One Device at a Time

To begin using solar electric power, start small with self-contained units that have all the components built in. Outdoor solar electric light/battery combinations are available in hardware stores and places like Target, Lowes, and Home Depot. They cost as little as $20 and can be installed simply by taking them out of the box and pushing the stake in the ground. Another way to begin small is with solar battery chargers for your small portable electronics. Simply set the charger in a south-facing window when the batteries need recharging.

Every device or appliance drawing its power needs from sunlight cuts its carbon emissions to zero. If everybody in the United

States charged their portable electronic batteries with solar power, we could take a whole power plant or two off line. This small start can make a difference, especially if we all do it. When everybody is stepping in the same direction together to accomplish something, that is the real giant step for mankind.

11

Doubling Up on Savings with Plumbing System Improvements

Check for Leaks

Our water as a utility or our water wells are often taken for granted in this country. Not too many of us have to walk a mile or two with a bucket to bring back a few gallons of potable water. Very few of us have to heat that hauled water with wood gathered from miles away when we want to wash a pan of dishes. So when our faucets leak a little we may tend to procrastinate about getting the tools out to change a faucet gasket or resurface the valve base where the washer contacts to shut off the supply. What's a little drip to us? The dripping faucet is not the only situation where your plumbing system's integrity is costing you money and wasting carbon energy. When the kids come in from outside for a cold drink of water on a hot day and run the water for 45 seconds to a minute to "make sure it's cold," that's a leak. When you get up in the morning to brush your teeth and run the hot water for the same 45 seconds or a minute to "make sure it's hot," that's a leak. When your water heater is burning gas or using electric power on and off over a 24-hour day to keep water hot just in case you need it, that's a leak, too. Your plumbing system leaks add up to bigger water bills, bigger gas bills, and/or bigger electric utility bills. Your home's plumbing system is one of the areas rife with low-hanging cash and carbon rewards that are ripe for the picking. You get double rewards from your efforts here: lower water bills and lower water heating bills. Save water, save cash—save hot water, save carbon!

Even those homes running well pumps will save twice on their efforts for making improvements to the plumbing system. Checking for leaks is no small thing, so let's begin.

Insulate Everything

To eliminate the water-is-not-hot-or-cold-enough problem, insulate all of your water pipes, both the hot and cold. Water coming in the house is cold, and insulating the cold pipes will help it stay that way. Use the prefabricated foam tubes or wrapping kits from your local hardware store—it is easy to install along pipes and is a job that nearly anyone can do. Insulate the hot water pipes starting right at the water heater and up to every faucet and appliance. Tape all the end joints of the foam together and along the vertical opening in the tubes. Your washing machine's and dishwasher's first loads will actually have warm water when it is called for by the control. Your dishwasher will do a better job, and you may be able to toggle off the heat boost button if your dishwasher has one. Cutting down on the running of hot water for testing when washing hands to just a few seconds will really make the savings add up.

Add Timers to Electric Hot Water Heaters

Using time-clock switches, coupled with relays if needed to handle the load, has the potential to save over 50 percent of your hot water heating bill. Gas hot water heaters may or may not be cheaper per BTU to run in your area, but they are far harder to control.

Replace Hot Water Heaters with One or More Electric In-Line Water Heaters

The photo below shows the "brains" inside an electric in-line water heater. This unit is unique in that it has a bit of built-in intelligence—a pressure switch—that turns the electric power on when the in-line water pressure drops when the hot water is

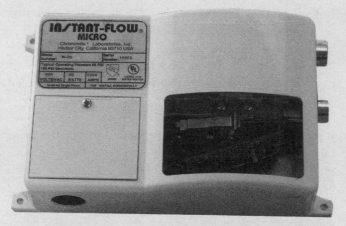

Photo Courtesy of Chronomite Laboratories, Inc., Industry, CA

turned on. In-line electric water heaters are among the greatest energy-saving appliances because they can be placed near or at the point of use, and they don't waste energy heating water when it's not being used. The installation of an in-line heater is much simpler than it was in the past. The newest fittings for connecting water supply pipes will work with copper or plastic and all you have to do is cut the pipe to length and insert it into the fitting. Because they work with copper or plastic, conversion points from one pipe type to another is simple. You can leave your existing hot water heating tank in place and use it for tempering (bringing to basement temperature) the water supplied to the in-line heater. If you do leave the old one installed, disconnect the power or cap off the gas supply and remove any insulating blankets on it.

Eliminate Outright Water Waste

Instead of using water sprinkler heads in the garden and around the shrubbery, install soaker hoses. Connect all outdoor watering hoses to timer controls, and run them in the early morning before the heat of the day can work to evaporate the water. Water timer controls are simple to install and available at most local hardware stores.

If you wash your car at home, convert your nozzle head to a fine mist type. You will use a lot less water. Do the same for inside shower heads. There is a vast array of fixed and handheld shower heads that can be set to fine mist to save on hot water use. The replacement of shower heads can be done with simple hand tools and takes very little time for a project that makes such big difference in energy use throughout the year.

Your savings with the insulation projects in this chapter will be hard to estimate and will take some time to notice, but they will save cash and carbon for many years into the future. By installing the in-line electric water heaters, your savings will begin to show up right away and add up quickly.

12

Harvesting the Savings from Green Technology Using Automated Controls

Getting Green with Envy or Green with Technology

You do not have to be a rich and famous celebrity to use advanced technology to help save energy in and around your home. The use of automation technology is beginning to gain more traction and is being installed during initial construction in many upscale buildings and spec homes.

How Technology Upgrades to Any Home Add Convenience and Save Cash and Carbon

How many times have you left a porch or garage light on, only to notice it casting shadows just as you are ready to slip into bed and begin dreaming about a greener planet? You say, "Oh well, I'll turn it off on my way to work in the morning." Then just as you slip under the sheets, your conscience gets the better of you and you trudge off into the cold to turn off the light, muttering to yourself, "I wish I didn't have to do this." There is a better way to deal with this and any and all situations where the lack of timely and adequate electrical controls leads to energy waste. The technology is there, it is not difficult or expensive to install, and you can get started doing it yourself on a very modest budget. Then you can grow the system of controls over time for more appliances, devices, and lights as time and money permits. Automated controls can save you that annoying walk to a light switch at night and can save large amounts of money on your electricity bills.

Automated Controls Fall into Seven Popular Categories

Manual Remote. Manual remote controls add a lot of convenience but require you to push a button or two to achieve control of lights or appliances. A typical installation includes an X10 control box plugged in and set in a convenient location. An X10 controller or switch is placed on all of the circuits you would want to turn off at night to save energy. One simply presses the remote controller's ALL/OFF switch, and all the controllers and switches that are programmed to that controller will turn off at the press of that one button. These are simple to install and the control unit can sit by the bed—all you have to do is plug it in to the wall outlet, and a number of remote switch modules can be controlled by it. You simply set a digital address on the switch modules so your controller can sync up with lights or appliances connected to the switch modules.

Timed. Timed controls have been around for a long time, and there are way too few installed in homes, apartments, and office buildings. Timed controls are simple to operate and fairly simple to install. There is a wide range of models, from simple ones that plug into an outlet to larger ones that have to be installed as a part of the home's wiring and controls. You can reduce a lot of the wasted heat going into a tank-style water heater or outdoor lights by running the circuit through a time-clock switch rated large enough to handle your electric load. Small cogs are placed on a 24-hour clock dial to throw the switch. One type of cog turns the switch off, the other type turns it back on. This type of control can ensure outdoor lights stay off during daylight hours. An electric water heater's electricity use can be curtailed by setting the water heater time-clock switch off at times when you are sleeping or no one is home. The savings can be as much as half or more of your electric water heating bill.

Local Passive. Sometimes called occupancy sensors, these are devices that use passive infrared, sound, or ultrasonic sound waves to sense the presence of a person. Local passive switches are typically wall mounted in residential applications. The photo on the next page shows a passive control you may find at a public washroom in a fast-food place. This same technology that automatically dispenses the towels there can control lights or other circuits in your home. Start by installing occupancy sensor switches in hallways, closets, and bathrooms, and watch the savings add up.

Event Driven. The best example of an event-driven switch, and the one that most people are familiar with, is found on automobile doors. When the door is open, the courtesy light in the car comes on and turns off right after or shortly after the door is closed. Door frame switches can work for closets, and automatic

sensing switches can be used over doorways to have lights come on as you are leaving the house. They will shut off after about 20 minutes of no activity.

Computer Programmable. This area of automated control has grown into whole-home automation. Computer software combined with control modules can control nearly every circuit in your house by setting the parameters of operation. In addition to the computer controlling your lights and appliances, you can add voice control and tell a particular light to turn on or off.

A computer loaded with smart home technology software, coupled with some X10 controls and a little bit of setup time, can go a long way toward harvesting savings in dollars and carbon contribution. Any light, appliance, or electrical device can be turned on and off and controlled on a timetable or by voice commands when set up with home automation software and X10 or similar controls. The computer will use an interface module to send control signals over the home's wiring to the controls.

You can buy a simple kit from Home Automated Living to get started with computer automation controls. The buy-in price for the basic kit is only $99, and the basic version of the HAL software includes one power line adapter module for sending the signal over your house wiring and one smart lamp module. The advanced software, giving you control over more types of devices, sells for $399. Check out their website at *www.automatedliving. com/shop/hal100b.shtml*. You will need a compatible computer and will probably want to buy the voice portal interface card for your computer.

Simple Logic Programmable. The programmable thermostats used to set back heating temperatures at night are examples of simple logic controls. They are designed for specific applications and provide a limited range of operating choices.

Light Sensing. You may remember the ads—back when utility companies advertised, promoted, and installed yard or security lights—with the simple slogan "on at dusk, off at dawn." Light sensor switch adaptors can be used on all outside lights to save energy when the light is no longer needed. All you do is simply screw the sensor switch adaptor into the light socket and then screw the lightbulb into the sensor. Light sensing switches are a simple and easy way to save on electrical energy. Light sensing switches can be combined with time-clock switches to further reduce energy waste and ensure a light is on when it is needed.

Calculating the Potential Savings from Automated Controls and Switches

Considering automated controls requires that you know some information about what you are controlling. You may have to estimate the amount of hours of wasted energy used without the automated controls. Knowing that the total wattage is 500 for outdoor lighting, every two hours of unnecessary energy use that an automated control prevents will save one kWh. Where I live, that is 15 cents saved on my light bill. If the control saves that every day of the year, the control would save me $54.75 in a year. Take the time to walk around your house and property with a notepad and find where you might be wasting electricity from lack of sufficient controls. If you install some controls, you might be amazed by the savings. Installing them can also lead to adding peace and tranquility for energy- and cost-conscious household residents.

The Future Look and Feel of Green Residences

Most Existing Apartments and Homes Are Energy-Eating Dinosaurs

Because of our lack of foresight in the past, we are stuck with a huge national inventory of apartments, homes, and structures of all kinds that barely give more than lip service to the idea of energy conservation. Sure, there are some energy-conserving homes, and there have been attempts at coming up with the ideal energy-conserving designs for homes, and there are many new products that cut our energy bills. But by and large, we are faced with a nation full of homes that must undergo significant modifications and upgrades, and projects like the ones outlined in this book are needed to nudge our domiciles down the pathway to significant energy conservation.

As energy costs continue to climb and the negative environmental impact of using more energy becomes more of a political and social issue, the effects will combine to drastically alter the way we view our housing alternatives. There is no doubt that high energy prices will begin to impact not only what is offered in new housing, but what we ask for and demand of builders and real estate developers.

As discussed earlier in the text, there at two distinct forks in the road to becoming environmentally responsible and fortunately, they are not mutually exclusive. The two path are to clean our environment (conserve nature) and to green our environment (reduce or eliminate the use of carbon-based energy). One would expect both to fully manifest in homes of the future. The building industry as a whole is slow to make changes and reluctant to fully incorporate modern technology. Much of this reluctance on the part of contractors is cost driven. New homes are still being built where the phone wiring is two pairs of wire twisted and run in a serial fashion from one phone jack to the next. This is somewhat ridiculous when you consider how much technology is typically used and supported in most homes. Consumers often do not know enough about the possible home construction options to demand more energy-saving or technologically advanced features for their money. Regrettably, we are still buying, building, and living in energy-eating relics.

Local and national green home building initiatives have frequently championed clean environmental building practices that limit waste streams and encourage recycling. In some areas, reducing water use will be of utmost importance. Indoor air quality is important to occupants and should always be of concern in every home now and in the future. These cleaner, more natural building initiatives are typically one-shot efforts that do pay dividends for years to come. They are worthy of doing, but the priority of action, effort, and investment should remain with long-term impacts.

Green and Clean Will Synergistically Combine in Homes of the Future

Low impact builds and clean, natural, and safe internal environments will be the order of day for new homes and apartments in the next decade. However, the two most important initiatives of future homes will still be shifting to renewable energy sources and drastically reducing carbon-based energy use through wise energy-consuming product choices. Energy-efficient homes will be built by design.

Incorporating low environmental impact building materials produced in the neighborhood will not be on most home builders' to-do lists until home buyers push back on the business of building as usual. It is sad to see Oregon- or Canada-sourced timber going into homes in my local area in Michigan, when there are a few competent lumber mills in the area, and millions of board feet of trees around us at their natural peak for harvesting. Local sandstone quarries have ceased operations, while concrete and building blocks are trucked in from hundreds of miles away. Hard rock left over from mining is plentiful locally but rarely if ever used in foundations or walls in new buildings. Copper lies in the ground here, while wire from copper mined in Chile or Africa is being installed every day. Iron ore is mined a hundred miles from my location but travels thousands of miles, burning up thousands of gallons of fossil fuel for transport, before it comes back in the form of building products.

Currently, sales of new homes are down nationally, as are sales of older homes. Perhaps this is a good time for the home building industry to take a collective breath and rethink some of the ways new homes are sourced and built. They should reconsider what materials to use and where to get them and take a long-term view of the pros and cons of every component, particularly the elements that consume or waste energy with current building practices. Home designs and construction that only meet minimum codes for required insulation are obsolete before they are even built from the green home buyer perspective. Energy-conscious home buyers should simply refuse to purchase such energy wasters and instead build new to an energy-saving design.

Public policy adjustments through legislation and stronger codes may be a way to encourage a major and more rapid shift toward energy conservation in homes of the future. Places where government can influence outcomes might include tightening building and remodeling codes, tax credits based on proven effective incorporation of energy-saving features, reduced-interest mortgage loans for energy-efficient homes, and even funding outright the demolition of houses and apartments that hold little promise to ever become energy efficient.

Green Homes and Apartments Will Be Redefined

At the risk of being criticized into time eternal, I am willing to put forth some prophecy, or—if you prefer—predictions, about what homes and apartment dwellings will begin to look like when all the oil and most of the natural gas and coal is gone. A pessimistic view of the future would have us back in our ancestral caves, living on rabbits and cooking and heating with wood. It is difficult to accurately predict, but a little conjecture of what might be is interesting and might evoke new thinking or discussion, which could lead to further inventions to save, eliminate, or reduce some of the carbon-based energy use now.

Unlike most of today's homes, green residences of the future will recapture and reuse as much energy as possible, and much of the energy will be converted on site from solar, geothermal, and wind. In the next few sections, we will consider how some of those new environmentally clean energy sources might be demonstrated in new home and apartment construction.

High Probability Energy-Related Predictions about Homes of the Future.
Energy consumption knowledge and practice *requirements* for home builders and remodeling contractors will increase through licensing and regulation. A large part of the licensure will involve demonstrated knowledge of energy alternatives and energy-saving features that can or must be incorporated within the home on new construction or remodels. Corresponding regulations will be placed on all subcontractors to maintain licensure through increased continuing education about energy reduction. Much of the continuing education across all trades will involve a new body of energy conservation laws and codes currently not on the books. Building contractors and their tradespeople will be mandated to use the latest in energy conservation products soon after they reach the market. Energy conservation laws will dictate that with each new construction, a per-person carbon footprint standard will be met or alternatively, the best-known

energy practices and products will have to be incorporated into the home. This will be necessary to receive an occupancy permit on new building or remodeling projects. Following are some of my predictions for future practices and products:

- **Earthwork** will be kept to an absolute minimum because of the cost to do it. Basements will rarely be built; most new home construction will be slab on grade. Many homes will literally be suspended above grade to limit positive or negative thermal bridging.

- **Concrete** will still be used, but only where necessary, mostly for overcoming weak soil strength. On-grade walks and driveways will be made from wood chips or locally obtained crushed stone or rock.

- **Masonry and stone** exterior walls and inside floors will increase in popularity because of their low to no maintenance features and thermal mass storage characteristics.

- Wall-to-wall carpeting made of **synthetic materials** will virtually disappear.

- **Metal framing** where readily available on a regional basis will become the framing material of choice. As more efforts are made to make homes more energy efficient, wood framing will give way to prefabricated steel and other metal components engineered to meet exact needs (strength, precision, durability). Steel and composite materials will become the framing materials of choice because they are clean and can be factory shaped to ideal specifications for optimum energy-conserving shapes that would be hard to duplicate with straight wood framing. Another plus of prefabricated metal framing is that it is easily assembled on site. It has fire resistant characteristics and can maintain strict uniformity to the needed dimensions for each project.

■ Energy conserving **homes** will be viewed as a generational asset, and people will pass efficient dwellings to the next generation.

■ Home **products** and production of a home's **components** will move closer to the home's assembly site, and production capacity for those components will develop on a regional basis.

■ Natural **wood** products will continue to be popular, particularly for furnishings, and a return to wood as a designer's material of choice will displace some of the **plastics** we currently use.

■ **Composite** materials will continue to be used, perhaps expanding because of the inherent synergy of combining dissimilar materials. Very thin sheets of stainless steel placed over and adhered to plywood bases are an example of this.

■ Future building codes will mandate **thermal protection** levels for dwellings far beyond what we would consider reasonable today. New high-tech materials made from natural sources will help achieve compliance to the codes.

■ **Moisture protection and vapor barriers** will be manufactured from more Earth-friendly materials. The need for them will decrease because of changes in construction methods and increased use of insulation.

■ Exterior **doors** will be thicker due to increased insulation and will present a much more energy-efficient profile. This will be true for outer doors and to some degree inner doors, where room-by-room temperatures are closely managed.

■ Exterior **windows** will be at least triple glazed, probably mandated by building codes to be gas filled and have polarizing properties.

■ For **finishes** and **fibers** used in homes, more natural products and options will win out over man-made ones.

■ **Equipment, appliances, and fixtures** will be energy efficient well beyond the Energy Star ratings in use today.

■ Quiet **blowers and vents** will be used to incrementally move heat or cool from room to room as occupants move about the dwelling.

■ **Clothes dryers** will use outside air and a miniaturized heat pump for drying. The heat from the clothes washer's waste water will help heat the clean water for the next load before being discharged down a drain. Combo units that wash and dry in one frame will replace the two separate units in most homes today.

■ Interior **furnishings** will also be made from more natural materials, with fewer plastics, polyesters, and products that are petroleum based. Real woods and fewer laminated or composite materials will become the preferred choice for home and office furniture.

■ National home building codes and local building requirements will mandate that all homes either meet a low-risk fire assessment standard or have **fire suppression** systems built in.

■ Standard **plumbing** will change to include things like air pressure–assisted flushing to reduce water use. Supply lines will be a slightly higher pressure and interior pipes and lines will be smaller and fully insulated to the point of use. Point-of-use, in-line tankless water heaters will become the norm in every home and building.

■ Every home requiring added heat and a dedicated **heating system** will have a ground source heat pump or an air source heat pump at the center of the heating system design. Closed loop heating systems will have underground zones as well to store excess heat in in-ground, salt-filled chambers. Furnaces and heating boilers will only be used in very large homes or apartment buildings.

■ **Ventilation** systems will always include a whole house air-to-air heat exchanger for supplying fresh air tempered by the exchanger to more closely match the desired indoor temperature.

■ Low demand **air-conditioning** systems will be heat pumps working in reverse, and not just dedicated cooling units. Where extra cooling is required a through-the-wall system will be used to supplement the central system or used by itself to cool only the occupied rooms.

■ The home's entire **electrical system** will be tightly managed and controlled by computer and digital automation to save energy in every possible way. Having some on-site electrical power generation will become the norm, not the exception, in homes of the future. No opportunity will be missed to capture energy from solar, wind, or rain and convert it to electric power. Every electronic device in the home will take advantage of miniaturization technology to reduce power consumption to an absolute minimum. Low voltage DC outlets will become common installation in homes to supply power to these power-reduced electronics. Power supply "bricks" will become collectors' items as vendors decide on a standard, low-power DC system, probably three volts.

■ All **communications** coming into and out of homes will be over small strands of fiber optic cable. Conversions to end-use signals will require very little power, and no power will be consumed when a communications device is not in use.

■ Home **exteriors** will be a combination of natural lifetime materials, such as stone and brick, and the exterior construction will be modified to integrate solar management.

The design of off-the-shelf photovoltaic panels and heat collectors will become more aesthetically pleasing and adaptable to all styles of architecture.

- **Utility** companies will still provide water, gas, and electric, but prices per unit will become very high as worldwide demand for energy increases and supplies from nonrenewable sources dwindle. A goal of 100 percent of energy from renewable sources will never be met. Nuclear-generated electric power will rapidly become the dominant source of energy as carbon-based energy sources dwindle to near zero.

- **Garages** will become smaller as more and more of our personal transportation becomes electric powered.

- **Factory-built homes** will be built out of lighter and stronger materials to reduce shipping weight and costs.

- As people travel or go on vacations, more consideration will be given to the energy footprint of the **unoccupied home**. Designs for new homes will include features where an unoccupied home will use only a tiny fraction of the energy used while it is occupied.

- **Walls, floors, and ceilings** will become thicker and will be built with designs and features to reduce unwanted thermal bridging, maximizing the use of thicker insulation material.

- Every new home will be built and wired for full automatic computer control of everything **electrical and mechanical** in the home.

- Homes will have Internet addresses under **IP6 protocol** so appliances and electronics can be monitored and controlled remotely via computer, PDA, or cell phone while the residents are on vacation or heading home on the daily commute.

■ A new-home-building **voluntary grading scheme** will emerge nationally that rates newly constructed homes on percentage of local content by cost and by weight, estimates of carbon used in transport and construction, cost per degree day for cooling and heating, relative rates of water consumption, and so on. Essentially and eventually the voluntary system will lead to a federal requirement for an **energy audit and disclosure statement** for every new or existing home sold or financed in the United States.

Low-Probability (but Still Possible) Energy-Related Predictions about Homes of the Future

■ **Steps and sidewalks** will capture energy from visitors' footsteps to supply energy to light walks and run doorbells.

■ The energy in falling **rain** will be captured and used to generate electricity for homes in high precipitation areas.

■ Every home will be built with combination air-to-air and ground source **heat pumps** to supply as much of the heating and cooling load as possible in the area.

■ Treadmills and exercise equipment will be built to **electrically capture human energy**, and that energy will be stored in batteries for later use to run small appliances. Run your two miles and get a piece of toast and jelly when you are done!

■ The sun always shines and generates heat, and vast areas on every continent have little to no vegetation or residents. Magnified solar arrays will collect light energy from collectors in these unoccupied areas. Instead of using or converting the energy collected there, it will be transported to points of use over **fiber optic cables**, where its light energy will be converted to heat and power systems where geothermal sources are not sufficient. Those same light collectors will provide light literally on the other side of the planet. As the Earth rotates and the sun lights up other light collectors, **fiber optic switching** will be used to divvy up the light to end points where it is needed.

A Few Final Thoughts

When a plant bud emerges from seed and appears from the ground in early spring, it is first nearly an all-white shoot that is hardly distinguishable as a plant. Then in a short while it changes to yellow with a tinge of green, and then finally in a couple of days it is bright green, growing steadily on its way to becoming a mature plant. When you embark on a plan to green up your residence, think of this example from nature with its slow but certain progress to becoming green. Map out your ideal energy-saving situations and goals for your home in energy dollars saved per month or year—or if you prefer, in annual carbon savings—and begin working steadily toward that goal, one project at a time. No matter how big or small the savings, achieving your goals will make a difference when the long-term future is considered.

From an excess carbon standpoint, the media and green community focus is currently on reducing the rate of accumulation and beginning to reverse carbon buildup in the atmosphere. To meet the inevitable, and perhaps final objective, it will become necessary *to manage the amount of carbon* in the air to a standard amount determined to be necessary for mankind's long-term benefit. The idea of managing carbon to some optimum level to benefit all people is not yet a common topic, but I believe it will become necessary for the long-term benefit of all living things on Earth. The Earth, as the craft that is moving mankind and all living creatures through the time and space of our universe, is filled with and supported by finite resources. Abuse or misuse of any one of them could accelerate our planetary downfall. As one dares to peek out past our natural lifetimes, there is no way to know if managing carbon in the atmosphere will become our collective salvation.

No one knows for certain if global warming is a good or a bad thing in the long run. The reality is that no one knows what Earth-born or space-born calamity may befall us, where the result is that the Earth is shaded by particles and cooled beyond any life forms' ability to survive, and life as we know it is totally extinguished from global freezing. If one thinks there is collective intelligence in all of nature, this period of global warming may very well be good. It is possible that it is happening now to ultimately save us from a future deep-freeze condition. If one believes that the natural order of things lacks an intelligence factor, and given all that could go wrong, there is a stronger argument for learning enough to become able to help nature along and manage our planet's average temperature to benefit humankind and all living things. No doubt much more knowledge is needed, and maybe a close call or two will befall the Earth and humankind before we get it right, but in this author's view getting to know the Earth is getting to love the Earth. Without fully seeking this knowledge, it is hard to call ourselves responsible stewards of the planet we call home. We don't usually want to hear about things that are off our current scientific and political radar screen, but that doesn't make them any less important.

No matter your current living situation—as apartment dweller, home renter, or homeowner—you can take responsibility for your own energy costs and by extension, your family's carbon footprint on the atmosphere. The projects and information contained in this book can become a first step in making a difference in your cost of energy and in reducing global greenhouse gases. Rise to the Kyoto Challenge and see if you can reduce your home's energy consumption by 7 percent (the U.S. goal component of Kyoto); if it does nothing else, it will save you money on your monthly utility bills.

There is more that can be done to save energy and many additional sources for further research and reading on the topic. For more information that we could not fit here, visit the author's website associated with this book at *www.gettingreducedenergy expenditurenow.com*.

Acknowledgments

Thanks as always to my wife, Penny, for her constant support and encouragement of my work as an author. Thanks to my agent, Carole McClendon, at Waterside Productions for her sage advice and counsel. Many thanks to Michael Sprague at Kaplan Publishing, for recognizing the value to the reader of getting straight-shooting information about the real potential savings in cash and carbon from truly green, energy-saving home improvement projects. My thanks to all the editorial staff at Kaplan for turning my sometimes rambling phases and thoughts into a book that can be read and enjoyed.

Index